AMERICA
IN THE
ECONOMIC
WORLD

AMERICA IN THE ECONOMIC WORLD

JOBS, NECESSITIES, AND ECONOMIC OPTIMIZATION

MICHAEL DOUGLAS GILBERT

LANGDON STREET PRESS,
MINNEAPOLIS

Copyright © 2014 by Michael Douglas Gilbert

Langdon Street Press
322 First Avenue N, 5th floor
Minneapolis, MN 55401
612.455.2293
www.langdonstreetpress.com

All rights reserved. No part of this publication may be reproduced, stored in a retrieval system, or transmitted, in any form or by any means, electronic, mechanical, photocopying, recording, or otherwise, without the prior written permission of the author.

ISBN-13: 978-1-62652-770-6
LCCN: 2014934982

Distributed by Itasca Books

Cover Design by Sophie Chi
Typeset by Mary Kristin Ross

Printed in the United States of America

For Deborah and Kathryn

For Rob, Brooklyn, and Eli

For Carolyn Sue

To elevate public discourse

Contents

Preface		xi
Acknowledgments		xvii
PART I	The Economic World	1
Ch. 1	A Perilous Existence	3
Ch. 2	A House of Cards	9
Ch. 3	Uneven Prosperity	15
Ch. 4	The Economic Problem of the Modern World	21
PART II	Economics and Finance	27
Ch. 5	The Fallacy of Composition	29
Ch. 6	Money and Banking	33
Ch. 7	Mortgage Lending and the Risk-Reward Trade-off	39
Ch. 8	Insurance	45
Ch. 9	The Financial Sector	49
Ch. 10	Entitlements and Welfare	57
Ch. 11	Lifetime Consumption	61
Ch. 12	Utility and the True Value of Money	69
Ch. 13	Taxation and the Two Welfare States	73
Ch. 14	Government Efficiency and Regulation	79
Ch. 15	The Business Cycle, the Great Depression, and Unemployment	85
PART III	American Economic History to 1981	95
Ch. 16	The Early Years and the Age of Delusion	97
Ch. 17	The 1970s: A Period of Transition	103
Ch. 18	The Age of Denial	109
PART IV	Ideology and Conflict	113
Ch. 19	Tax Cuts, Distribution, and Redistribution	115
Ch. 20	Lessons of War	123

Ch. 21	Reagan, Bush, and Clinton	135
Ch. 22	George W. Bush	143
Ch. 23	The Great Recession	151
Ch. 24	The Causes of the Great Recession	159
Ch. 25	Barack Obama	169
PART V	America's Problems in Context	181
Ch. 26	The Global Economy	183
Ch. 27	Economic Optimization	191
Ch. 28	The Politics of Economics in America	199
Ch. 29	Pay the Bills	207
Ch. 30	One Nation, Divisible	217
Final Thoughts		223
Endnotes		233
Selected Bibliography		243
Index		247

Preface

This book offers a new and refreshing view of economics. It discusses the difficulties of obtaining necessities in a modern, complex economy, the success of nations in an era of economic globalization, and the relationship between government and the private sector. The book includes a history and analysis of the impact of ideology on recent public policy decisions in America. It presents just those economic and financial concepts necessary to understand current events. *America in the Economic World* is an original contribution to social science intended to encourage sensible public policies.

A unique feature of the book is its straightforward exposition. It is intended for social science professionals and students, but it is readily accessible to any adult reader. The largely self-contained presentation allows everyone easy access to the relevant topics in economics, finance, and history necessary to form their own opinions on critical issues. The book contains no mathematics beyond the simplest arithmetic. There are no graphs or charts or tables of numbers.

In 1968, on the recommendation of a friend, I took my first course in economics. I was intrigued by an academic subject that had such obvious practical applications. As a mathematics major who would go on to work for decades as a geophysicist, it would have been easy for me to fall into the same trap that many technically trained students of economics have succumbed to; namely, the view that economic life is fully explained by--even determined by--graphs and equations. But life's experiences told me otherwise.

One particular point raised in that 1968 economics course has always stayed with me. The impressive standard of living that we have had in the United States can be attributed to the high compensation that Americans receive for their greater productivity. But that naturally raises the question: if Americans make so much more money than people in other countries, then how can Americans compete with that cheaper labor? The answer given in 1968 was: it is not just the cost of labor that matters. The quantity and quality of capital equipment that the labor is combined with also determines workers' productivity. It was clear in 1968 that there could be a big problem if that capital equipment ever became available to countries that had cheaper labor.

I have always been interested in how people obtain necessities for themselves in a complicated world. Years of studying economics and finance have only reinforced my opinion that it will be more difficult in the future for large numbers of people in advanced industrial societies to find adequate jobs. The neat mathematics of economic theory may be cold comfort to those left out of the global economy. We must always remember to ask the question: do people eat *before* or *after* the supply and demand curves cross?

In the 1970s, the United States sold grain to the Soviet Union, our Cold War enemy. Americans reasoned that someone would sell them grain, so why shouldn't our farmers make some money? Since I had a keen interest in economics, I followed this closely in the newspaper. I learned that a combination of reduced grain supplies and higher energy costs were driving up the price of beef in the United States. On a trip to the supermarket late on a Saturday afternoon, I saw this interesting economic phenomenon for myself. As I walked beside the meat counter, I noted that not only were beef prices higher, but chicken, pork, and seafood prices were higher as well. These were what economists call "substitute goods," and their prices all moved higher at the same time.

As I compared prices, I noticed the only other customer at the meat counter. She was a woman in her forties who looked like she had just gotten off work and was shopping for her family. At one point I saw her standing about ten feet from the meat counter, motionless and staring ahead, almost catatonic. For me, a young man with a good job, higher meat prices were an inconvenience, and they were an affirmation of what I had learned in my study of economics. For this woman, they represented a very real danger that she could not afford enough protein for her family. I have never forgotten that look on her face.

It is an inescapable fact of life that we are part of an interconnected economy in which people do not provide necessities for themselves. They usually buy them from businesses that are part of a complex system of production, distribution, and sales. The primitive economy of farms or log cabins in the wilderness in which people produced all of the necessities of life for themselves is long gone. To provide for oneself and to be a good citizen, it is essential to understand the relationship between the market economy, public policies, and the means by which ordinary people obtain necessities in the modern world.

This book provides an analysis and overview of economics, finance, and history. Part I (chapters 1–4) discusses global economic development with special attention given to things that are important today such as jobs and international competition. It addresses the difficulty of maintaining full employment in a complex economy as well as what historically advanced countries such as the United States must do to compete in the modern world. Part II (chapters 5–15) is a unique presentation of selected topics in economics and finance, all of which have direct applications to current events. It provides new insight into such familiar topics as Medicare, Social Security, mortgage lending, regulation, education, unemployment, and public infrastructure. Part III (chapters 16–18) covers the economic history of the United States up to 1981. These three chapters help readers understand the factors that have shaped our concept of the American Dream.

Part IV (chapters 19–25) analyzes the impact of ideology on both domestic and foreign policy decisions. This section also brings the study of American economic history to the present day. Chapter 20 covers American military history from 1941 to 2011. Not only are wars great economic events, but studying the impact of ideology on decisions to go to war helps us to understand the uses of ideology in determining domestic economic policies.

Part V (chapters 26–30) discusses America's problems in light of current politics and in the context of information provided in the first twenty-five chapters. In the final section, I offer some thoughts on the state of economic theory, and on people's misconceptions about government.

Throughout this book, whenever I return to previously discussed information, I indicate the referenced chapter in parentheses. This is not intended to insult the intelligence of experienced readers, who will easily recall these topics. It is meant to remind people that facts and analysis do come from somewhere. This technique emphasizes that this book is not engaged in the shoot-from-the-hip discussions currently seen on television where several people talk loudly and simultaneously. Readers will easily get used to these chapter references in parentheses.

It is now critical that Americans apply the lessons of economics and history to correct failed public policies and avoid burdening future generations with past mistakes. It is my hope that people can gather insight while reading this book that will allow them to form their own honest opinions. My intention is to provide important information and analysis, to encourage sensible and compassionate policies, and to elevate public discourse.

Acknowledgments

Several people I know deserve recognition. Robert McGuire and Scott McGuire have contributed their technical expertise to solving the often thorny computer problems that invariably arise in the modern age of high technology.

Doris Ashbrook generously provided important suggestions that improved the book. I also appreciated her belief that the book is important.

The editors and staff at Langdon Street Press introduced me to their high publication standards and offered suggestions that significantly improved the book.

Above all, I wish to thank my daughter, Kathryn McGuire, who persistently prodded me to write. Without Kathryn's help and encouragement, this book could not have been written.

Part I
The Economic World

The woman who answers the toll-free number of a well-known hotel chain is pleasant and chatty. She meticulously checks and rechecks my reservation information, spelling every word to me for verification. The process takes over twenty minutes, much longer than my previous experiences with this reservation system. I finally realize from her slight accent and the background noise that she is at a foreign call center, probably in India. It is far less expensive for the hotel chain to pay for twenty minutes of her time than to pay an American for ten minutes.

A young man in Texas has worked as a clerk and a laborer at discount stores and home improvement centers, but he has taken computer-aided drafting courses at a community college. A friend in the telecommunications field tells him that the industry often uses computer draftsmen in the Philippines and India. Companies can send specifications of physical facilities and receive completed drawings over the World Wide Web. While there are often communication problems, both technical and cultural, the labor is cheaper overseas where workers will do computer-aided drafting for about the same compensation as the minimum wage in the United States. Those foreign workers are the young man's competition.

Any trip to the store reminds Americans that we are part of a global economy. Everything from food to toys to electronics is likely to come from another country. It is almost impossible to find clothing made in the United States. Even the fruits of American ingenuity such as new electronic gadgets produce more jobs overseas than at home. People seeking work are part of a vast worldwide labor pool. They all need money to provide themselves with necessities since very few produce their own food, clothing, or shelter.

The economic world we live in is the product of many centuries of development. But, now, the entry of millions of new workers into the global economy may have as great an impact on the historically advanced nations of North America and Europe as on the newly emerging economies themselves.

Chapter 1
A Perilous Existence

About ten thousand years ago, our primitive ancestors began systematic agriculture in areas of the world blessed with favorable soil and climate. They were able to domesticate wild plants and animals and thus dramatically increase food production. This development freed excess workers to engage in ostensibly non-agricultural occupations such as making pottery, leather goods, and metal objects. An agricultural surplus allowed the formation of cities and the explosion of goods and services we now enjoy.[1] But people in the newly created urban areas paid a price for these advances; they were now separated from the production of necessities. They could not eat pottery or leather goods.

The economic world still strives to produce more with less labor. In the eighteenth century, mechanical devices such as James Watt's steam engine replaced massive amounts of human and animal labor. A century later, the "Father of Scientific Management," Frederick W. Taylor, began studying how specific tasks were done in the workplace and determined ways to do them more efficiently. Taylor's work lives on in the modern field of production and operations management. Henry Ford's assembly line would combine machines with job design to dramatically increase automobile production. Advances in electrical devices—analog and digital—would bring consumers everything from radio to television to computers. Now, people can hold more computing power in their hands than NASA used on its Apollo moon mission.

People assume that new jobs will always be created to replace those lost by advances in technology. Economic history since the beginning of the Industrial Revolution has largely been the story of new product development, new industries, new types of employment, and ever-increasing production. But this development took place almost entirely in the historically advanced countries of Europe and North America. During this time, the undeveloped parts of the world were just sources of raw material and primitive labor. Small countries in Europe, such as England, France, Holland, Portugal, and Spain, acquired resources by establishing colonies around the world. The United States effectively colonized itself as American settlers took land from Native American tribes. However, by the late twentieth century, formerly undeveloped countries like South Korea, China, India, and Brazil could use advanced technology and their low labor costs to enter world markets. Americans could now lose their jobs to globalization as well as to advances in technology.

The world has never needed everybody to work. Even our most primitive ancestors provided for children and for the old and injured, at least temporarily. Today, nursing home residents, incarcerated criminals, and wealthy people who choose a life of leisure are all provided for despite their lack of participation in the work force. In general, the number of consumers far exceeds the number of producers, especially in the more prosperous nations of the world. There is no inherent equality between the number of people who need to work to support themselves and the number of people the economy needs to produce all the goods and services demanded by consumers. Countries that have recently entered the global economy may have more flexibility in dealing with this mismatch. These countries can more easily move workers back and forth between industrial work in cities and their inefficient agricultural sectors. If ten people can work in a rice paddy, then so can twelve. But how many people in Manhattan can go work on a farm if there is high unemployment in New York? Globalization and technology almost certainly guarantee that in the historically advanced countries of the world, the number of people who need jobs to support themselves will be greater than the number of people needed to produce the goods and services those countries consume or export.

The Development of Money

The use of money and the development of a large, complex financial sector have had a profound effect on the economic world. Initially, goods could only be exchanged by the clumsy process of bartering. The development of money as a medium of exchange greatly facilitated trade. Moreover, money's use as a store of value allowed the accumulation of wealth without the need to amass physical assets. Since labor could be paid for with money, people could work in activities far removed from necessities and use their earnings to buy necessities. Thus one could be a teacher of philosophy or maker of gold jewelry and yet still provide oneself with food, clothing, and shelter.

The use of money was so successful in facilitating trade and other economic activity that a financial sector developed that loaned money (for delayed payments), held savings (for delayed purchases), and later processed financial transactions (for contemporaneous purchases). When stock corporations were created to accumulate money for capital-intensive development, the financial sector would handle equities (shares of stock) and allow business entities to borrow and save money. The financial sector would grow to such size and complexity that it would create its own self-contained economic activity. One could bet money on trade or anything remotely related to trade, insure an activity, or even bet money on money. The financial sector would grow to seemingly have a life of its own.

This overview of economic development provides a foundation for understanding the complexities and dangers of the modern world. Soil and climate only offer a first approximation to the distribution of economic success in the world. Many other factors from innovation to hard work to good fortune come into play. A country in an agriculturally favorable region can be a financial disaster due to poor government (Zimbabwe), while an undemocratic country with terrain hardly conducive to agriculture can attain great wealth due to the presence of natural resources (Saudi Arabia). A small, highly-populated nation with limited natural resources can use value-added production to prosper (Germany).

A few people in undeveloped countries can benefit greatly from a local niche of the larger global economy. Meanwhile, some people in highly advanced countries may have little or nothing to offer the world, and there may not be much opportunity in the domestic market if their country lags behind its global competitors. Both individuals, and their nations, must consciously compete with all other countries of the world by making investments in business, education, and infrastructure. Otherwise, even nominally prosperous nations may find themselves overrun with impoverished citizens. No matter what a country's form of government, democratic or not, this failure to invest in the future could lead to massive political and social upheaval. In an interconnected world economy, billionaires are the same everywhere, millionaires are about the same everywhere, the middle class is becoming the same everywhere, and unfortunately, the poor may become the same everywhere also. One day, the reference point for poverty even in advanced countries like the United States may not be the "genteel poverty" of the first half of the twentieth century. It may be the poverty of the third-world. What would keep poor Americans from being as poor as poor Haitians?

Necessities in the Modern World

The definition of "necessity" has expanded in modern societies. Since people now must rely on jobs to make money for everything they need or want, transportation to work ranks with food, clothing, and shelter as a necessity. Physical security, including national defense and police and fire protection, is essential. And people who suffer from painful or deadly health problems may not be able to work. Therefore, medical care is also a necessity.

An important lesson of economic history is this:

humans have been separated from their ability to provide themselves with necessities. Virtually no people in modern, advanced economies produce their own food or their own clothing or their own shelter or their own health care or their own transportation or provide for their own physical security, let alone all six. We pay for those necessities by making money doing work, but there is no reason to believe that a job will be there for us. The old adage that "the world does not owe you a living" has taken a new meaning. We don't envy our primitive ancestors their short, brutal lives. But we must learn to solve the problems of our complex, job-based society to prevent the creation of a large underclass of unemployed citizens who lack primitive man's options to provide for their most basic needs.

Chapter 2
A House of Cards

One consumer's spending is someone else's revenue. Our purchases provide money for suppliers of goods and services who in turn pay their suppliers, their employees, and themselves. As this process continues, money spreads through the economy with the well-known "multiplier effect": one dollar spent may ultimately produce two or three dollars in economic activity. A modern economy provides both frivolous and desperately needed goods and services. The golf club salesman uses his income to buy bread while the baker's income may allow him to buy a diamond bracelet from a jeweler who needs money for medical care. Our purchases are determined by our needs, wants, and financial resources. Unless we are poor, we assume that we will be able to buy the necessities of life. We tend to notice flashier things—diamond rings, fine cars, and meals at fancy restaurants—while taking for granted bread, socks, and dental check-ups. But in an economic downturn, job loss or the fear of reduced income forces people to carefully consider each purchase. We then notice that the things we buy fall into three categories: necessities, deferrable necessities, and luxury items.

We have already noted that the definition of "necessities" has expanded beyond food, clothing, and shelter to include security, transportation, and medical care. Some would argue that, in our modern society, access to a phone is also essential. A job search is difficult without reliable communication. So we may define a necessity to be a good or service whose omission will eventually produce significant negative consequences.

At times, lack of financial resources may force us to spend less or find cheaper substitutes. We may eat meat less often or replace it with cheese or beans. Many purchases of necessities may be deferred for long periods of time. Clothing life can be extended. Even mediocre furniture will last a surprisingly long time. Home repairs may be delayed for years. However, some deferred purchases of necessities may have disastrous consequences. Eliminating dental care can lead to infection and even heart disease. Neglected auto maintenance prevents the detection of bad brakes or worn tires. But even necessities become deferrable necessities when people have no money.

Luxuries vs. Necessities

A luxury is any good or service not necessary to sustain life or to enable the work necessary to sustain life. Tools for a home hobby are a luxury but tools needed for work are a necessity. Most things we buy are luxury items: jewelry, tennis rackets, most electronics, fancy food, manicures, alcoholic beverages, theater tickets, and much more. No one has to go on a vacation, and you can go your whole life without eating in a restaurant, even a fast food restaurant. If necessary, a barber or a hairstylist can be replaced by a pair of scissors and a comb.

Much of the work in our economy is devoted to the production of luxuries or deferrable necessities. A country can withstand large-scale and long-term loss of jobs without jeopardizing the production of necessities and many of the jobs lost need never come back. Thus the modern economy is a "house of cards" with much, if not most, activity dependent on prosperity and not need. Prosperity allows for many optional jobs providing luxury goods and services. This underlying fragility of the economic system is often disguised, especially in a severe downturn when millions of jobs are lost. The job losses appear to be simply an adjustment to a lower level of output. But the downturn may be prolonged by the elimination of much optional activity.

The Importance of Jobs

When we consider what we really need to survive, a job or source of income ranks below only oxygen and water as necessary to sustain life. Food and other necessities are usually bought with income from a job. Society should welcome any opportunity for jobs deemed useful. In the public sector, infrastructure repair and construction, law enforcement, and national defense require tax payments. These are all not only essential services, but they have the additional benefit of sustaining the economic life of workers and their families. In the private sector, employment is determined by consumer demand. Jobs consist of a wild mix of brain surgeons, manicurists, sales clerks, golf pros, auto mechanics, and fortune tellers. Nevertheless, these jobs support people and their families.

When millions of jobs are lost in an economic downturn, the multiplier effect of their spending is largely lost as well. This creates a "negative multiplier effect," which is not an economic event so much as the loss of many potential economic events. This further adds to unemployment and further decreases consumer demand. Since there was previously adequate production of goods and services and now demand is reduced, there is no reason to believe that these people can be easily absorbed back into the work force.

It is worth noting that massive employment occurs in certain areas (e.g., criminal justice, national defense, dental hygiene) that we may wish were not necessary. But if these huge sources of employment did not exist, where would all these people work? For example, at the end of 2009, there were over 7.3 million adults on probation or parole, or in jail or prison in the United States.[1] This supported millions of jobs for law enforcement, prison guards and wardens, probation and parole officers, judges, court employees, prosecutors, defense attorneys, private prisons, suppliers to prison systems, and support personnel for all the above functions. Neither the people in these jobs, nor the prisoners incarcerated in state and federal prisons, provide any significant amount of goods or services other than criminal justice itself, yet all of these people have their needs met either as prisoners or from their income.

To understand the fragile nature of an economy, consider a world in which these jobs didn't exist. If there were no crime, few of these people would be needed in the economic system. In fact, the lack of consumption by people in the criminal justice system would eliminate the need for many other jobs. Output would shrink. Any tax savings would be needed instead to fund the increased demand for government services due to the huge increase in unemployment.

Fortunately, this is just a hypothetical case. There is plenty of crime in society to employ or incarcerate all of these otherwise unnecessary workers. But if certain drugs were legalized resulting in a dramatic decrease in the prison population, unemployment could go up significantly. Social services would be needed for newly unemployed criminal justice employees, and this would provide some jobs, though not for the ex-prisoners. Ironically, crime itself helps provide the necessary equilibrium in the job market.

The inexorable trend in economic history is that a smaller and smaller proportion of the population is needed to provide necessities for those people who can afford them. Over the years, the expansion of what we consider to be a necessity has created many jobs. But only widespread prosperity allows the existence of the large number of jobs that produce luxuries and deferrable necessities, and those jobs need not be in the United States.

Chapter 3
Uneven Prosperity

What determines whether or not an economy thrives? Fortunate geography has given some places in the world an advantage in agricultural production. Some countries may derive revenue from exporting nonagricultural natural resources. Other countries, like Taiwan, have only their peoples' labor to offer the world. This suggests several models for economic activity:*

- The Natural Resource Model describes countries where the main source of income is selling their minerals (oil, natural gas, aluminum ore, copper ore, etc.) or agricultural output, often through companies from more developed nations. This model typically applies to third world countries where only a small, well-connected portion of the population prospers. In extreme cases like Saudi Arabia, there is such an abundance of resources that everyone's standard of living can be elevated, although income distribution there as elsewhere is a big issue. Many oil and agriculture exporting nations fit this model.

---

* The economic models presented here describe in general terms how nations interact with the global economy.

    These models are neither mutually exclusive nor jointly exhaustive. For example, a country can offer both low-cost labor and natural resources. Some countries may not fit any of these models. Impoverished nations may interact with the world only as recipients of foreign aid. The world doesn't need everyone to work.

- In The Low Labor Cost Model, the natural resource offered is abundant, cheap labor instead of minerals or agricultural products. Even skilled labor is cheap in these countries. China and India have used this model in the last few decades to enter the global economy.
- The Value-Added Model uses highly trained, skilled labor to produce valuable products such as automobiles, tools, and electronic goods that often command a premium price. After the destruction of World War II, Japan, Germany, and many other countries moved toward this model. They recognized that offering only low cost labor to the world would not allow a very high standard of living. Japan, for example, made plastic toys and trinkets in the 1950s but by the 1970s the country produced high quality automobiles, electronics, and steel products.
- The American Business Model is unique and is presented here only for historical purposes. Over the years, the United States has combined abundant natural resources, both cheap and skilled labor, episodic creativity, readily available financing, and advanced management skills to mass produce a wide variety of products at competitive prices in a largely self-contained economy. In chapter 16, we will see how the economic history of the United States has affected every American's opinion of how the economic world is supposed to work.
- The Global Business Model draws on the entire world's resources to duplicate the American Business Model. Entrepreneurs at a company may use

financing from anywhere in the world to send raw materials to nations with cheap labor to produce newly invented products in a process overseen by the best available management talent. The revenue may accrue to the benefit of many countries. In some countries, a great many people may earn low wages from this process, while elsewhere a handful of people may make a great deal of money. The United States, Canada, the United Kingdom, Japan, Germany, France, and all the most advanced countries in the world use this model. Much of their domestic economic activity is determined by their degree of success with this global model. A persistent trade deficit may indicate that a nation is not holding its own in global markets.

The Impact of Globalization

Nations using the Natural Resource Model or the Low Labor Cost Model strive to attain the Value-Added Model, but they may find opposition from companies and countries that profit from exploiting their resources. More and more, economic activity in China and in India approximates the Global Business Model. Government efforts in China to maintain low labor costs by keeping the currency artificially low-valued in foreign exchange markets create domestic inflation and a demand for higher wages. In time, their highly skilled workers will demand the higher compensation that value-added jobs provide. China and every other country in the world are potentially at the mercy of the next new low-cost nation on the global scene.

With the exception of a few unusually resource-rich countries, the successful nations of the world will all eventually follow the Global Business Model in their trade with other countries. Free trade policy will prevent countries from shielding themselves from global competition. As was suggested earlier (in chapter 1), global economic equilibrium will produce a world in which billionaires, millionaires, the middle class, and the poor are the same, respectively, in countries throughout the world. Without conscious government policies to encourage education, training, jobs, and an economic safety net, the population of even the most successful countries will be an uneasy mix of those who prosper globally or domestically, and those who are left out. The world will tend toward a global economic equilibrium that incorporates everyone.

People often follow a stock market index, such as the Dow Jones Industrial Average or the S&P 500, to gauge how well their economy is doing. But in recent years, many international corporations have become less dependent on their home countries as they compete in global markets. Companies across the globe will sell to whoever has money to buy their goods and services. Corporations domiciled in nations with 30 percent unemployment can thrive. A business's priorities are not affected by patriotism; its allegiance is only to its shareholders. Therefore, even aside from the impact of greed, businesses and people may tend to see themselves as participants in a global economy. They may thus easily disassociate themselves from the economic concerns of their fellow citizens, and this lack of concern may permeate the political process.

Meanwhile, the least economically successful countries often have population sizes that far outstrip their limited resources. This includes Haiti and some countries in the Horn of Africa such as Somalia and Sudan. Foreign aid only provides short-term relief. These countries may attempt a Low Labor Cost model, but birth control, more stable government, and foreign investment will be needed for long-term economic improvement.

Of course, there are many non-economic factors that are critical for economic success.

Functional and stable government, respect for the rule of law, a national commitment to education and training, a healthy population, and recognition of the sanctity of contracts, copyrights, and trademarks are all important.

Expanded Uses of the Economic Models

The economic models can also serve as reference points for people, companies, or subdivisions (e.g. states) within nations. Globalization increasingly requires Americans to ask themselves what they have to offer the world. Americans may need more education and training to earn money from value-added work. Otherwise, they are merely cheap labor competing in world markets. And while there are many different forms of business activity, it is reasonable to ask whether a business could suffer from inadequate supplies of input resources or could lose its customers to foreign competitors with cheaper labor. Can a company add so much value in quality or so many extra features to its product that the product commands a higher market price? Can a business compete in world markets, or is it inherently a domestic or local business?

States, too, have very different amounts of available resources. For example, over the last century, Texas has been the Saudi Arabia of the lower forty-eight states in the United States. Oil and natural gas have funded much investment in the state in a wide variety of areas including education, medicine, technology, infrastructure, and banking. While it takes a great deal of skill to find and produce hydrocarbons, you cannot find them if they are not there. Is Texas wealthy because it is economically successful, or is it economically successful because it is wealthy? If Rhode Island or Maine had Texas's oil and natural gas resources, which state would be the most prosperous?

Ultimately, we can conclude that for people, companies, states, and nations, economic success requires having something to offer the world. In fact, "prosperity," or what economists might call a comparative advantage, can make any economic system or any economic entity (person, company, state, or nation) look successful. But we cannot ascribe noneconomic virtues based solely on economic success. Saudi Arabia doesn't have the world's best government because of its great wealth. Alaska is not the best-run state because of its high per-capita oil and natural gas revenue. Rich people are not inherently more worthy than poor people. Luck is an uncontrollable economic variable.

Chapter 4
The Economic Problem of the Modern World

Hundreds of millions of people in large countries like China, India, and Brazil now compete directly with workers in North America and Europe. They earn money for necessities, often by producing luxuries or deferrable necessities. Meanwhile, many people in the United States, Japan, and Europe have found that the world's uneven prosperity (chapter 3) no longer works to their advantage. Many jobs have gone to other countries. Businesses in free-market economies will outsource jobs to save money, use automation and mechanization to lower costs, and avoid investments in sluggish economies, including their own. But how do advanced nations in a global economy overcome the powerful forces causing unemployment?

Employment in the Global Economy

Economics is defined as the study of the allocation of scarce resources to various alternative uses. If enough people are willing and able to pay enough money, a product will be made available for sale and they will be able to buy it. So the problem of maintaining employment in an advanced economy can be phrased as follows: how is a scarce resource (jobs in the global economy) allocated to alternative uses (many job seekers)? Those job seekers willing to pay enough will get the jobs. How do job seekers "pay" for a job? They accept lower wages, or they offer greater skills, or they exhibit greater productivity.

But vocational skills can be created in low-wage countries with on-the-job training. Productivity is determined largely by investments in capital equipment (plants, machinery, and computers) and by advanced management and production techniques, all of which are exportable to low-wage nations. Ultimately, many job seekers in advanced countries must compete with lower wages to "buy" jobs. However, a country that maintains employment by accepting these low wages will have less money for consumption. This hurts private sector businesses and thus requires fewer jobs to meet domestic demand. The "negative multiplier effect" (chapter 2) takes over. Gross Domestic Product is lower, as are tax revenues. The nation becomes poorer.

In the starkest terms, human beings need oxygen, water, and a host of necessities typically paid for with income from a job. The global economy offers these necessities, and even luxuries, in abundance. But the change in global economic equilibrium caused by the entry of many new countries in recent years has profound implications for the employment level in countries with traditionally higher labor costs. Now, the proper study of economics in the modern world is this: how does a country create useful employment in order to provide enough jobs to allow the allocation of necessary goods and services to those otherwise without the means to pay for those necessities?

This is a problem of highly developed countries, since unemployment will increase as jobs there go to lower-wage countries. In addition, there are two other reasons these countries should be concerned about long-term increases in unemployment. First, the historic trend in economic development (chapter 1) is increased efficiency, which eliminates jobs—but competition in the global economy may leave the newly unemployed with less job opportunities. Second, many workers produce luxuries or deferrable necessities (chapter 2). Their jobs may easily be lost in an economic downturn, but may not easily return.

In general, there is no reason to believe that everyone who needs a job will have a job even in the most advanced economies. People may find themselves unemployed amid plenty. If an eco-system didn't provide enough oxygen or water, it would be deemed a failure. Likewise, if an economic system doesn't produce enough jobs, many people will consider it to be a failure. Since market forces may cause permanent net job losses in historically advanced economies, those countries must proactively address the problem of increased unemployment.

The Importance of Public Sector Employment

In the competitive global economy, the private sector alone may be inadequate to provide enough jobs. The only employment a country can control and increase is public sector jobs. Any need in society can be viewed as an opportunity to give someone employment. If something is broken, hire someone to fix it. If something is dirty, pay someone to clean it. In education, some students require tutors or special instruction. All students benefit from enrichment programs in art and music. Expanded pre-K education can pay off dramatically. An aging population requires more health care. Expanded social services improve the quality of life for many people. New recreation facilities provide the public with inexpensive activities that promote good health. Everyone benefits from well-maintained public infrastructure.

It is neither necessary nor desirable to invent "make-work" projects to create jobs. Nations have many unmet needs. Allocating resources to increase employment is a win, win, win, win, win proposition. People with jobs take care of themselves, private sector businesses benefit from increased consumption, economic investment increases, tax revenues increase, and demand for welfare services decreases. The unemployment rate alone is not sufficient to measure how well an economy is functioning, since some people may be left out of the statistics. Researchers cannot easily distinguish between those who have given up looking for a job, those who have started engaging in black-market or illegal activity, people who win the lottery, and those who suddenly inherit a lot of money.

It is important to note that any economy, including a free-market economy unfettered by government, can reach economic equilibrium at any level, including zero. Some people may object to this notion and argue that there is a lower limit beneath which economic activity will not go since people must have certain necessities. But consumer demand, whether for necessities or anything else, requires that a person be both willing and able to buy a desired good or service. No matter how much you may want a four-hundred-foot yacht, you have no economic demand for the yacht if you cannot afford it. No matter how much you may need a loaf of bread, you have no economic demand for it if you cannot afford it.

Part II
Economics and Finance

In the 1990s, a middle-class family in Texas decided to take a chance and do without health insurance. Both husband and wife worked, but neither of their employers provided group coverage. When one of their teenage sons hurt his leg, they took him to a hospital emergency room, where an X-ray confirmed a serious injury. They were referred to an orthopedist and told that their son would probably need surgery. Contrary to popular opinion, not all health problems can be solved at an emergency room. All the Texas family got was an X-ray, some crutches, a preliminary diagnosis, and a big bill. When they called the orthopedist's office for an appointment, the first question they were asked was "Who is your insurance carrier?" The costs of surgery would virtually bankrupt them.

A young nurse works for a primary care physician who mainly sees adults over fifty years old. She explains that due to lack of adequate reimbursement, he no longer takes new Medicare patients unless they are in one of the two Medicare Advantage plans he accepts. She says that these plans are very cost-conscious and tend to be picky about every medical service the doctor provides. This makes both her job and the physician's job more difficult. Unlike most people her age, this woman in her late twenties is on the front lines of an American health care dilemma: how to provide adequate health insurance to senior citizens. People in their twenties tend to see themselves as invincible, so it is hard to convince them that they will need health care or retirement income in the future. But this young nurse says that people should be willing to pay more for Medicare throughout their lives because it will be so important to them later.

Americans have often found themselves in the middle of national economic and political issues that they prefer to encounter only on the nightly news. Their problems may have occurred because of some loss: of a job, of health insurance, of their savings, or of their home to foreclosure. Economic terms like "recession," "stimulus," "unemployment," "tax cuts," and "mortgage backed securities" swirl around them and require explanations. Both social scientists and ordinary readers will appreciate the unique view of economics and finance presented in the next eleven chapters. We discuss only topics that are necessary in order to be an informed citizen. The next chapter reminds us that we must actively seek economic knowledge, since our own experiences can mislead us.[*]

---

[*] The chapters in part II include many elementary concepts in economics and finance that may be found in numerous textbooks. Some useful references are included in the bibliography. Part II also includes original insight and clarifications.

Chapter 5
The Fallacy of Composition

In September, 2005, Hurricane Rita was in the Gulf of Mexico and aimed directly at Houston, Texas, America's fourth-largest city. Hurricane Katrina had devastated portions of the Gulf Coast on August 29 and was fresh on people's minds.[1] Everyone in the mandatory evacuation zones near Houston readily packed up and left. These zones were near the coast or in low-lying areas prone to flooding. But many people who lived far out of the evacuation zones also tried to leave. They were fearful of being stuck for weeks in the hot Houston summer without electricity to power their air conditioners. With too many people clogging the roads out of town, nobody went anywhere. Interstate 45 to Dallas and US 290 to Austin were literally parking lots as six- and eight-lane highways eventually narrowed to four or even to two lanes. Cars became overheated and people ran out of gas. Hurricane Rita largely bypassed Houston to the east but more people died on the highways than from the storm.

This event illustrates a concept known as the Fallacy of Composition. Just because a certain course of action (leaving home ahead of a hurricane) is good for you, does not mean that it is still a good idea if too many people do the same thing. When Hurricane Rita threatened Houston, people in mandatory evacuation areas could not get to safety because other people chose to unwittingly clog the roads. Later, in 2008, Hurricane Ike struck Houston directly but there were comparatively few problems for the people who had to evacuate the area. Residents outside the evacuation zones had learned their lesson and stayed home.

The Fallacy of Composition is a very general concept with both economic and noneconomic applications. It is often phrased as follows: examining only one part of something may not indicate the nature of the whole. A blind man cannot deduce the shape of an elephant by examining the trunk alone. Usually the concern is whether we can use the results of one person's choice of action (a small part of overall human activity) as guidance for deciding many people's actions (the whole of human activity). The following economic examples will illustrate this further.

It is a good idea for people to have savings. It may protect them from future calamity, or allow them to buy an expensive item some day. But if everyone saves more, the lack of consumption in the economy may reduce overall economic activity and cause a recession. This phenomenon, called the Paradox of Thrift, is an example of the Fallacy of Composition.

A rancher decides to raise more cattle in order to take advantage of high beef prices. If all ranchers do the same, the beef market will be inundated with cattle, beef prices will decrease, and the rancher could actually lose money.

In a severe economic downturn, a businessman would naturally try to cut costs to compensate for lower sales. He might reduce employees' hours and allow attrition to reduce staff. He might even lay off workers. It would also be prudent to reduce inventory and close less-profitable locations. All of these decisions make sense in a shrinking economy but the cumulative effect of many thousands of such decisions only makes the downturn worse. Consumption would decline because people would have less income. Manufacturers would also produce less due to reduced consumption. Government would have lower tax revenues because of a decrease in overall economic activity. Any reduction in government spending due to lower tax revenues would compound the problem of reduced consumption. The "negative multiplier effect" (chapter 2) would hurt the economy. The businessman's choices are understandable, but are an example of the Fallacy of Composition. In a very natural way, a free market economy in a severe downturn works in reverse to cause an economic implosion. This can only be corrected by a renewed cause for optimism or by some external force that reverses the pattern of self-serving behavior.

A fundamental premise of free-market economics is that if everyone acts in his own economic self-interest, then the economy will prosper. But the Fallacy of Composition reminds us of the possibility that many personal choices could sum up to a national economic disaster. As long as there is more than one person in the economy, self-serving decisions may have unanticipated consequences.

Chapter 6
Money and Banking

Anyone who asks "What is money?" is invariably told stories about seashells, gold and silver, cigarettes in a World War II prisoner of war camp, or other such objects historically used to facilitate trade. The use of these items merely produced an advanced form of bartering. The exchange of an object (furs) for another object (corn) was made easier by the introduction of a third object (gold or seashells). This early money was useful because it had the characteristics we now associate with modern money. It was a <u>unit of account</u>, since its per-unit value (an ounce of gold or a large, pretty seashell) was understood to be relatively fixed compared to objects whose values fluctuated with supply and demand. Because this money had value for its own sake, it was accepted as a <u>medium of exchange</u>. Also, money was a <u>store of value</u> because it was much easier to hold in large quantities than stacks of furs or piles of food.

The Gold Standard

Since gold was universally prized for its beauty and scarcity, many countries adopted a gold standard. They issued gold coins, or currency and other coins backed by gold. As the world economy expanded, more money was needed for commerce but there was no reason that inadequate gold supplies should restrain economic activity. Thus the intuitive notion that all money should be backed by gold gave way to the gold-reserve standard, in which countries could issue sufficient money to support economic activity and only use gold to settle imbalances in international trade. But imbalances in trade between countries and the need to settle debt obligations could produce massive outflows of gold that thwarted a country's desire to maintain its currency at a certain fixed gold exchange rate. In September, 1931, for example, the Bank of England was losing as much as $80 million of gold a day before it went off the gold standard.[1]

Eventually the world's financial system recognized that it made more sense to let the forces of supply and demand adjust the value of a nation's currency. When the United States was on the gold standard, it needed to maintain gold supplies, so it imposed restrictions on the purchase of gold by ordinary citizens. Ironically, when the United States had a gold standard, one could not easily convert money to gold. But now that it is off the gold standard, any American can simply buy gold with his money.

The modern monetary system does not depend on gold or any other asset for its value. It is backed by "the full faith and credit" of the government. Modern money "works" because you can buy things like gold with it. The relative value, or exchange rate, of different currencies is determined by the demand for each currency. A country could try to maintain its money at an artificially low value in order to make its products cheaper in international trade and thus gain a competitive advantage. However, this policy would create inflation in that country since imports would be more expensive.

Because large transactions, such as purchases of businesses, buildings, and cars, are made with checks or electronic transfers, most money in the United States is held in institutions as electrons in a computer. The amount of coinage and currency in circulation fluctuates with demand. This amount typically increases before Thanksgiving and shrinks after New Year's Day in order to accommodate holiday shoppers. At any given moment, at least 85 percent of money in the United States is just entries in a computer. It is represented by neither coins nor currency nor gold.

Commercial banks make money by lending their depositors' money. They also make money on fees they charge their customers. In a vibrant, healthy economy, banks can make a good profit from lending despite their higher cost of funds (i.e., higher interest paid to depositors). They may reduce fees to attract more depositors. In a sluggish economy, there are fewer good lending opportunities so banks place more emphasis on fees. Also, they earn proportionately more money acting as financial service providers to their customers.

It would seem that if a bank pays, say, one-fourth percent annually for deposits and loans money at 6 percent, there is a good profit to be made. But in addition to the substantial costs they must bear for buildings, equipment, labor, and so on, the banks have much more to lose if someone defaults on a loan than they will gain if the loan is repaid in a timely manner. In the previous example, a $100,000 loan at 6% interest costing the bank one-quarter percent would yield a gross profit of $5,750 annually, before other costs. But a default would cost the bank $100,250 after a year, and it still must pay those other costs (building, equipment, labor). Banks must lend money prudently, since they have so much to lose in case of default.

Money Creation by Commercial Banks

Commercial banks increase their lending and their potential profits by lending more money than they have in deposits. This is possible, and perfectly legal, due to a concept called fractional reserve banking. If a bank is required to hold only 20 percent (or one-fifth) of its deposits in reserve, the remaining 80 percent is available for lending. In the banking system as a whole, a $100,000 deposit requires $20,000 in reserves and allows $80,000 in lending. This $80,000 (which may be put in a bank other than the original lender) requires that $16,000 in reserves (20 percent) be set aside and this allows another $64,000 in lending, and so on. It can be shown that with a 20 percent reserve requirement, an initial $100,000 deposit could produce $400,000 in lending. This increases the total money in the banking system from the original $100,000 deposit to $100,000 plus $400,000, or a total of $500,000.[2] Thus commercial banks literally create money.

Many things affect the nation's money supply, including actions by the Federal Reserve System and borrowing by the US government. But the money-creating capabilities of commercial banks allow them to respond in a routine way to lending opportunities that exist in the economy. In our sophisticated financial system, all deposits contribute to this lending capacity. The bank holdings (checking accounts, certificates of deposit, etc.) of rich and poor people alike, and of both large and small businesses, make lending possible. In a fairly automatic way, a prosperous economy makes more money available for lending. Likewise, a sluggish economy with fewer good lending opportunities produces a natural contraction both of lending and of money in bank deposits.

This discussion suggests two other important observations about the banking system. First, banks use depositors' money to increase their assets (loans) and their liabilities (the deposits of borrowers) without increasing the owners' equity in the bank. Thus banks, and financial institutions in general, are highly leveraged businesses, meaning they have little cushion, or "skin in the game," if something goes wrong. Non-financial businesses typically have a proportionally greater net worth to protect them from disaster. After the financial collapse in 2007 that produced the Great Recession, these highly leveraged financial institutions were in much worse condition than non-financial businesses.

A second observation is that the flimsy nature of most money as mere files in a computer combined with banks' abilities to lend money beyond the amount of their deposits, strongly suggests that close government supervision of banking is necessary to preserve the sanctity of the money supply. We don't want bankers to create money by simply feeding electrons into their computers.

Chapter 7
Mortgage Lending and the Risk-Reward Trade-off

Banks must be prudent when lending money because they are primarily using other people's assets (their depositors') and because they have much more to lose if a borrower defaults on a loan than they have to gain if he repays the loan (chapter 6). Banks should routinely confirm a prospective borrower's income, credit score, assets, liabilities, and capacity to repay a loan.

While each borrower may be unique, one lending principle is constant: long-term loans are riskier than short-term loans. For loans with terms of about one year or less, it is reasonable to assume that a borrower's capacity to repay the money will remain unchanged. For intermediate-term loans, collateral may be necessary. For example, a bank could repossess a car if a three- to five-year auto loan were not repaid. A large home improvement loan might be backed by a second mortgage.

Avoiding Risks in Mortgage Lending

Very long-term loans, such as fifteen- to thirty-year mortgages, are inherently risky. Today's millionaire buying an expensive home may be a pauper in ten or fifteen years and the bank won't know about it until he misses a payment. Over a long period of time, lots of things can change, so mortgage lenders need to be especially careful. They require a down payment or private mortgage insurance, an accurate appraisal of the home to be purchased, and, of course, a clear title to that home, since it will be collateral for the loan.

Over the years, banks and other financial institutions held their own mortgage loans as assets, which gave them a special incentive to be careful lenders. But this subjected them to another type of lending risk called geographic risk. Since their loans were made to borrowers living in the vicinity of the bank, a downturn in the local economy created the specter of numerous home loan defaults. The creation of securitized mortgages solved this problem. Home loans could be sold, often in pieces, into various pools of mortgages, and each pool would be a financial instrument that could be sold all over the world. The mortgage lenders could buy and hold these securities as assets, thus achieving geographic diversity in their lending portfolio. Since American homes provided collateral, these mortgage-backed securities were historically considered to be some of the safest investments in the world. The extra liquidity received from investors meant that more money was available in the United States for home loans, thus making it cheaper for Americans to achieve their dreams of home ownership.

The creation of mortgage-backed securities also made it possible for lenders to make imprudent loans and dump them onto the financial sector. However, this was frowned upon for two reasons. Such a lender would be a pariah in the banking community for creating "bad paper," or loans not likely to be repaid. Secondly, it was considered unethical to mistreat borrowers by making loans that they could not repay. After all, the borrowers were the bank's customers and hurting them damaged the entire community.

Financially, prospective borrowers come in all shapes and sizes with vast differences in incomes, assets, liabilities, credit scores, and repayment histories. Some may be deemed "prime" borrowers, since all the information on their loan applications is positive. Others may be considered "subprime" borrowers due to poor credit scores, perhaps because of a history of missing loan or credit card payments.

In practice, a bank may have a difficult time comparing different lending opportunities when all information is considered. For example, which of the following is the higher-risk borrower?

- A single, twenty-nine-year-old assistant manager of a discount store with no debts and a high credit score wants to buy his first home for $80,000. He makes $36,000 a year, has $10,000 in savings, and a five-year-old car worth $9,000. He has no dependents.

- A married, forty-six-year-old dentist has two children who no longer live at home. He is self-employed and purchased his dental practice five years ago from a retired dentist. He and his wife can sell their current home for $200,000 and net $110,000 after repaying the mortgage, and after paying real estate fees and other expenses. They could then put at least 20 percent down on the $320,000 home they want to buy. His personal income (business income minus business expenses) is $120,000 a year. He has a poor credit score due to his inability to pay credit card companies a few years ago when his children were in college and while he was paying for his dental practice. That business was paid for and his credit card debts reduced from nearly $50,000 to about $10,000 when his wife inherited some money. They have $5,000 in savings.

The bank's loan officer will likely recommend both loans to management. The dentist's loan will be labeled subprime because of his poor payment history and low credit score. As a subprime borrower, he may pay a higher interest rate and may be required to put more than 20 percent down. But which borrower is the greater risk? The retail manager will have very little savings after he buys the house, and if he loses his job in a poor economic environment, it is unlikely that he could make as much money elsewhere. The dentist owns his business outright and his dental practice is well established.

The Risk-Reward Trade-off

Why would a bank even make a subprime loan? This is explained by the most fundamental concept of finance, the risk-reward trade-off. If one wants a low-risk investment, it is necessary to accept a lower return. On the other hand, if one wants the possibility of a higher return, it is necessary to accept higher risk. This risk-reward trade-off exists because people tend to act rationally. They will compete for low-risk investments and drive up their prices, thus lowering the return. All other things being equal, people will be less eager to buy into higher-risk investments. This reduces their prices thus allowing a higher return. Viewed another way, people or companies with good credit ratings are considered to be less risky borrowers and will pay a lower interest rate for a loan than higher-risk borrowers.

Interestingly, the risk-reward trade-off provides two criteria for detecting financial scams. It is inherently suspicious if someone claims to have a low-risk, high-return investment opportunity. It is also suspicious if they are seeking numerous investors each with relatively small amounts of money. If a low-risk, high-return investment actually existed, it would be possible to get huge amounts of money from any one of numerous knowledgeable investors.

In the financial world, this well-known risk-reward trade-off allows us to list prospective investment opportunities from higher-risk, higher-return investments down to lower-risk, lower-return investments as follows: (1) so-called penny stocks, often of new companies with limited histories, (2) blue-chip stocks, (3) corporate bonds from blue-chip companies, (4) bank certificates of deposit, and (5) United States Treasury Bills. Other financial securities can be placed in this list based on their particular risk-reward characteristics.

With this in mind, it is easy to see why banks and other mortgage lenders would offer subprime mortgages. The banks are attracted to the higher returns on these higher-risk investments for the same reason individual investors might choose to put their money in common stock rather than certificates of deposit. And as long as a distinction is made between securitized mortgages containing only high-quality (prime) loans and those containing subprime mortgages, investors in securitized mortgages can make a rational choice based on the risk-reward trade-off principle.

Chapter 8
Insurance

Mortgage lenders require that borrowers have homeowner's insurance in order to protect the lender since the home is collateral for the mortgage loan. Typically, one-twelfth of the annual premium for this insurance is added to the loan repayment (principal and interest) in each monthly note. This money is kept in an escrow fund and used to pay the annual insurance premium on the home.

The Importance of Insurance

Obtaining homeowner's insurance is a requirement for getting a mortgage loan. But at other times, people aren't told what to do and whether out of ignorance or naivety, they may opt out of buying important insurance protection. The following anecdote illustrates how dangerous this can be.

A woman we shall call Mrs. Smith was widowed after her husband died unexpectedly. When she received his life insurance proceeds, she wisely used most of the money to pay off her mortgage. Mrs. Smith had a good job and believed that having her home paid for would provide security for her and her teenage daughter. But when she paid off the mortgage, she no longer had anyone forcing her to get insurance. She never paid another homeowner's insurance premium. When her house burned down, it was uninsured, and she was forced to move into an apartment with her sister.[1]

Insurance can provide important protection against financial disaster that may occur after a sudden event like a fire or an automobile accident. It can also be used to help pay for frequently occurring costs like medical care. An often overlooked feature of some medical, dental, and prescription drug insurance is that the insurance company's ability to negotiate discounts can significantly reduce the cost of services. It would not be unusual for an insured patient to save more money from the negotiated discounts than from the actual insurance payments to providers.

Private sector companies offer insurance protection in exchange for premiums with the expectation that they will make a profit. Their decision to offer insurance is guided by what we may call the Insurance Principle: Insurance can be provided to cover certain losses if they occur so infrequently that it is possible to offer affordable premiums that more than cover the insurance company's expenses.

Affordable premiums are important since they allow the insurer to cover many people. The premiums collected from the multitude can be kept in reserve to pay the claims of the unfortunate few. Although tangible goods are often bought with insurance proceeds, insurance companies are considered to be providers of financial services.

What if people don't have certain kinds of critical insurance? Maybe they can't afford it, or they decide to take a chance, or for some reason, insurance companies won't provide it. If an uninsured person suffers a loss, it is tempting to say, "Too bad. They made a poor decision.

Perhaps friends and relatives could help them." But over a large population, the effects of many such uninsured losses could hurt the economy for a long period of time.

The National Flood Insurance Program

Some places are prone to flooding, such as coastal regions along the Atlantic Ocean and the Gulf of Mexico, as well as areas near certain rivers, like the Mississippi. To protect their collateral, mortgage lenders may require borrowers in these areas to have flood insurance. But private insurance companies don't want to offer flood insurance in these places since that would violate the Insurance Principle. Flooding in some places is not infrequent. Worse still, these floods may be monumentally expensive, since they often occur over a wide area. If there is no insurance available, what should be done? Should the 100 million or more people in these areas simply take a chance on financial ruin? Or should they abandon these flood-prone areas and live elsewhere? That would make a large part of the country uninhabitable.

Fortunately, Congress solved this problem by creating the National Flood Insurance Program, now a component of the Federal Emergency Management Agency (FEMA). Established by the National Flood Insurance Act of 1968, this program offers flood insurance in exchange for state and community compliance with flood plain management regulations that are designed to prevent or minimize flooding.[2] While there is controversy when this insurance pays repeated claims on the same structure damaged in multiple flooding events, this program is deemed to be a better alternative than forcing millions of Americans to pack up and leave their homes.

It is natural to ask, since a free-market economic system cannot provide a much-needed service like private flood insurance, are there other services for which this economic system is inadequate? The answer is yes, and it turns out that the list is quite long. If a country had to rely solely on a free-market economic system unfettered by government, it would not have national defense, homeland security, police and fire protection, or universal public education. Sometimes government must provide the service of accumulating public money via taxation to pay private contractors to create tangible output such as roads and bridges (public infrastructure), which would not otherwise be available.

The private insurance industry receives many billions of dollars in premiums and holds money in reserves to pay claims. Individual insurance companies may protect themselves by purchasing insurance from so-called reinsurance companies. The insurance industry tries to increase its assets by investing the money either directly in specific projects such as residential or commercial construction, or in financial products such as stocks and bonds. Insurance and other insurance-like financial activities are important parts of the financial sector.

Chapter 9
The Financial Sector

The real economy is made up of businesses that produce either tangible goods or non-financial services. The financial sector is made up of businesses that offer financial services and financial products. This sector is often referred to as "Wall Street," or the "paper economy." Governments provide services, such as defense or police and fire protection, and also provide a mechanism to accumulate money for the construction of public infrastructure, such as roads and bridges. Non-profit organizations (charities, churches, foundations) may offer both services (counseling) and tangible goods (food for the needy).

Most people encounter the financial system at commercial banks where they have checking and savings accounts. Commercial banks also offer loans and retirement accounts. Other financial sector services include insurance (life, medical, home, auto), brokerage (buying and selling stocks and bonds), and financial advice (when customers must make insurance, brokerage, or retirement choices). Businesses use the financial sector for routine transactions or to help sell their bonds or common stock.

More exotic financial products, such as derivatives or option and futures contracts, are not uncommon, but ordinary bank customers are unfamiliar with them. At any given time, these products cover trillions of dollars in transactions worldwide. They are used by sophisticated investors either for insurance or speculation.

Commercial banks may seem to be quite labor-intensive, with all their tellers, account executives, and loan officers. But a feature of the financial sector that distinguishes it from the real economy is that financial firms handle very large amounts of money for the number of employees they have. It typically takes more workers in the real economy to produce goods (such as cars or food) or to provide services (medical care or plumbing) than it does to handle "paper" financial transactions. For example, a company in the real economy may need 4,000 employees to produce $5 billion in gross revenue, while a financial firm that does derivatives, options, or brokerage work may handle $100 billion in financial transactions annually and produce $5 billion in gross revenue, but need only 2,000 employees. Advances in technology make the financial sector particularly susceptible to the long-term trend in the world's economic development (chapter 1) of needing fewer people to do more work.

Economic Investment vs. Financial Investment

Economic investment is money spent to increase output. Specifically, it is money spent on (1) tools, equipment, and machinery; (2) construction of buildings; or (3) inventory for resale. It is important to note that when we "invest" in the financial sector, we are typically not making an economic investment. Buying stocks or bonds is merely a change of ownership of an asset. Even when a company "goes public" and offers stock for the first time in an IPO (initial public offering), this only produces a change in the ownership of an existing firm. In some cases, stock may be offered to raise money for economic investment in lieu of borrowing money or using internally generated funds. But when people invest in the financial sector, they are not usually investing, in an economic sense.

We must recognize this important and long-standing distinction between economic investment and financial investment. Economic investment may quickly create new output and new jobs, as well as future output and jobs. For example, building a manufacturing plant requires workers and materials for construction. Once the plant is finished, other workers will use equipment and raw materials to produce output. In contrast, financial investment is merely the movement of money and the change of ownership in existing assets and financial products.

Money used for consumption maintains jobs in the economy, produces business profits, generates tax revenue, and induces economic investment. Financial investments in pension funds and retirement accounts are to be used for future consumption. But too often, Wall Street only provides mechanisms for non-productive wealth accumulation. Increased income disparity between wealthy people and ordinary people, great inheritance, and lower tax rates, allow a small portion of the population to use income from financial investments to effectively disassociate itself economically from most Americans.

American companies can make money all over the world but they may not spend it in the United States. In the economic downturn that followed the 2007-09 recession, large American corporations had amassed $2 trillion in cash, some of which might eventually be needed to pay off debt. Meanwhile, they saw no opportunity to economically invest. They also chose not to make this money available for consumption by distributing it to shareholders or employees. So where do you put $2 trillion to keep it from benefitting the economy? In the global financial sector, of course. But how does Wall Street—or the international financial sector for that matter—absorb so much money? In general, money can go into one of three types of financial investments:

- Fixed-income investments, such as bonds or certificates of deposit, earn interest. As long as interest rates can go down, financial firms can hold increasing amounts of money in various fixed-income investments simply by lowering interest rates. It costs the same amount of money for banks to pay 0.25 percent interest to hold $4 trillion as it would for them to pay 0.50 percent interest to hold $2 trillion. As the US economy collapsed in 2008, businesses, non-profit organizations, and wealthy individuals cheerfully accepted virtually zero percent interest to put huge sums of money in US Treasury Bills, the safest of investments.
- Equity investments are ownership shares of corporations. As more and more money is put into equities, share prices increase allowing the stock market to absorb even more money with the same number of shares. So one million shares at $20 per share will tie up $20 million, but the same one million shares at $50 per share will tie up $50 million. On the other hand, if stock prices go down, large sums of money can be lost in the market.
- Over the years, Wall Street has created several other types of financial instruments which are also used for purposes other than consumption or economic

investment. These financial products include call and put options, futures contracts, and derivatives. These allow investors to either speculate on or insure real economic activity, without participating in the real economy. Businesses may hedge to protect themselves from price increases in raw materials, or from price reductions in commodities they sell. Speculative activity, such as betting on oil price increases or on a stock price decrease, may produce a self-fulfilling prophecy if enough money is bet the same way. Wealthy individuals can participate in these exotic activities by investing in so-called hedge funds. These are mutual funds with great flexibility to invest or speculate in worldwide markets.

There is virtually no limit to how much money can be put into the financial sector without contributing to useful activity in the real economy. No jobs are created. No economic investment occurs.

Derivatives

Each year there are hundreds of trillions of dollars in derivative transactions worldwide. A derivative is defined as a financial instrument whose value depends on something else. Typically, a derivative is a financial product designed to protect the purchaser from some kind of loss. However, a derivative is never referred to as an insurance product, since that might subject the derivative industry to various insurance laws—including the requirement that it hold reserves.

An example will illustrate how a derivative might be used to "insure" business activity.

Derivative Example: A corporation we shall call X-corp earns $50 million a year processing a plant grown in Asia into a finished product for sale in the United States. This has been a profitable business for years. But X-corp has one concern: crop failure could occur if high temperatures during a critical three months of the growing season caused a drought. This would cause a lower yield and jeopardize X-corp's profits. Although this event is unlikely, X-corp will protect itself by buying a derivative product offered by Wall Street. The derivative would pay X-corp $25 million in the event that the average temperature at a long-standing weather station was higher than some average defined in the derivative contract.

This is an insurance contract for X-corp. The counterparty offering the derivative is willing to risk $25 million for the critical ninety days in the growing season in order to make money insuring against an unlikely event. Notice that this derivative is tied to, but outside of, the real economy. And potentially anybody could take X-corp's side of this derivative transaction even though they are not participating in X-corp's industry. Note also that only X-corp is protected by this derivative. Neither the Asian growers nor the ultimate consumers of the finished product will get any relief if there is a crop failure due to high temperatures.

Another quick example of a derivative is quite revealing. At the height of the 2008 financial crisis, a large insurance company was in danger of failing. But those holding that company's debt could avail themselves of a derivative product for protection against default. At that time, "it would cost investors $612,000 to insure $10 million of ... debt every year for the next five years."[1] Thus risk is eliminated for holders of one financial product (bonds) by using another financial product (derivatives).

Several important observations can be made about the modern financial sector:

- The international financial sector can absorb massive amounts of money without producing jobs or any real economic activity.
- Advanced financial products like derivatives may undermine the notion of risk as the rationale justifying a high return on capital. Now it may be possible to engage in certain business activities with the expectation that one will either make a profit or be protected in the event of a loss. *Heads, you win! Tails, you don't lose!* The risk is shifted to those offering derivatives.
- Any mechanism such as tax cuts that increases discretionary income for high-income people is likely to remove money from the real economy and direct it to the financial sector. Tax cuts thus produce a drain on the real economy comparable to sending money overseas by buying imports. This is an even greater problem in a recession when both domestic consumption and economic investment are badly needed.
- Wealth accumulated in the financial sector allows a small portion of the population to live an economic life separate from their country's real economy. They can be provided for by financial investments often taxed at lower, long-term capital gains rates without ever having to personally produce goods or services, or to be economically productive in any way.

Chapter 10
Entitlements and Welfare

We expect people to work in order to make money to buy necessities (chapter 1). But what about young children whose parents cannot provide for them? Decent people expect these children to be taken care of irrespective of their parents' problems. The Fallacy of Composition (chapter 5) warns us that just because some children may routinely be helped by family, we can not assume that all children will be cared for. In a large nation, systematic provisions must be made to tend to neglected children. Helpless young people are entitled to some minimum level of care.

Elderly people routinely suffer the loss of physical and even mental abilities as they get older. Society must acknowledge that, at some point, these older people may not be able to take care of themselves. Similarly, people in the prime of life may suffer sudden misfortune that renders them incapable of work or even unable to care for themselves. After an automobile accident, a quadriplegic who has been discharged from the hospital cannot just be wheeled to the side of the road with the expectation that the invisible hand of the market will take care of him.

An <u>entitlement</u> is a necessity provided by government that people cannot be expected to provide for themselves.

While there may be honest differences as to what a necessity is, every American is the beneficiary of numerous entitlements, including national defense, homeland security, police and fire protection, public infrastructure, and the judicial system. These public goods are just as much entitlement as the services of government agencies for the young, the old, and the unfortunate.

A person may never need the help of the police, the fire department, or agencies that help the elderly, but it is reasonable to expect all of these services to be available. Adults are no more capable of providing themselves with homeland security or roads and bridges than a five-year-old child is capable of taking care of himself.

In contrast, <u>welfare</u> is a necessity provided by government that people are normally expected to provide for themselves.

People in the prime of life—older than children and not yet suffering from the effects of old age—are expected to work, make money, and pay for their needs. So when do you provide welfare to people? Some decisions are simple. If a nation's economy is so sluggish that many people are out of work, food stamps may be needed to keep people alive. Charities such as food banks and churches with food pantries are not able to systematically provide food every day for tens of millions of people nationwide.

Other questions are more complicated. How poor do people have to be to receive welfare payments? If no jobs are available in an area, what are people expected to do when they reach some lifetime limit on receiving welfare? As the following examples illustrate, it may not always be easy, or even necessary, to make a distinction between entitlements and welfare.

Example 1: A flood destroys a town of 5,000 people who lose everything, including their jobs. Are the resources people receive considered entitlements? Flooding is rare in their part of the country. Or are those resources a form of welfare? They could have bought flood insurance or accumulated savings in case of an emergency.

Example 2: A three-year-old child needs food, clothing, and shelter because her unemployed, single mother has no resources. The child is entitled to care. Should we simplify the mother's job search and eliminate her day care expenses by taking the child from her? If we leave the child with the mother and help the mother financially, is the mother getting welfare or an entitlement?

If a country simply doesn't need every healthy person in the prime of life to work, should the unemployed be provided with necessities by government? If not, and if many of them have no one to turn to for help, wouldn't we expect them to resort to scavenging, black market activity, and crime? It may be less expensive to deal with them by offering assistance. Their consumption is useful to businesses even if we don't need them for any productive activity.

Chapter 11
Lifetime Consumption

We now turn our attention to how people pay for necessities when they do have financial resources. If we go to the grocery store for a loaf of bread, we can pay by cash, check, or debit card. These are immediate payments, at least compared to paying by a credit card, a delayed payment that may incur finance charges. Unlike bread, expensive purchases cannot typically be paid for immediately.

In general, people pay for things in three different ways:

- <u>Contemporaneous payments</u> are used to buy now and pay now. We make use of money we have now, whether in the bank or on our person.
- <u>Deferred payments</u> are used to buy now and pay later. Big-ticket items such as houses, automobiles, furniture, and major appliances are often too expensive for most people to pay for contemporaneously.
- <u>Prepayments</u> are used to pay now and buy later. These are used to pay toward future large expenses that we are not likely to have enough money for when they occur. Some insurance falls into this category. Small amounts paid annually for life insurance may pay relatively large benefits if a person dies. So-called 529 plans allow people to accumulate funds to pay the future college expenses of their children or young relatives. Before credit cards were offered

indiscriminately, banks encouraged "Christmas club" savings accounts in which their customers saved all year to have enough money for the expensive holiday season.

When people make a purchase with deferred payments, they must include these payments along with contemporaneous payments in their budget. Because they buy a car or other expensive item today, their future spending must be reduced in order to allow deferred payments. This is also true for businesses, non-profit organizations, and governments. Future spending may be limited by previous purchases that are still unpaid. To pay off existing debt and avoid incurring additional debt, government must receive more revenue (from taxes, fees, assessments, etc.) each year than it spends on the services it provides that year.

People find it easy to incur contemporaneous and deferred payments, since in both cases they get the satisfaction of buying something now. A much more difficult issue is purchasing future necessities that are so expensive they require prepayment. For example, nursing home care and even in-home care can be very expensive. Very few people can pay for this care contemporaneously. Long-term care insurance is offered by many companies, but most people don't buy it.

Medicare

What about retirement medical insurance? Unlike long-term care, anyone who gets old enough will almost certainly incur medical expenses. For the overwhelming majority of older people, Medicare or some other government insurance program is the only health insurance available. There are four reasons that private companies don't offer primary health insurance for senior citizens:

- Such insurance violates the Insurance Principle (chapter 8). Health problems are the norm, not the exception, among the elderly. Everyone who is sixty-five or older has a preexisting condition that has always led to death, often at great expense. That pre-existing condition is being sixty-five or older. For health insurance purposes, the elderly represent adverse selection, (i.e., a population of undesirable customers). This explains why the private health insurance industry does not use its extensive congressional lobbying resources to advocate the elimination of Medicare so that "the free-market can handle it."
- Elderly people cannot pay for late-in-life health insurance because their income is reduced and the premiums would be prohibitive. Therefore, compared to providing health insurance for younger people who make near-contemporaneous insurance payments, retiree health insurance is not feasible. Very few people would be able to afford it.
- If Medicare were replaced with private sector coverage and there were no government involvement whatsoever, people would have to make the same prepayments they make now for Medicare throughout their lifetime, plus the amount their employers now pay to Medicare, plus

enough to make up for current Medicare shortfalls, plus enough to cover the profits and advertising expenses of private companies.
- If people had to use a private sector company for retirement medical insurance, they would have to pay for many years before they were actually covered. But would the company they chose still be in business when they turned sixty-five? Suppose the company offering the best plan in 1985 was Enron Health Insurance.

The Medicare Advantage program illustrates the problem of artificially injecting for-profit companies into an inherently unprofitable activity. Like traditional Medicare, these insurance plans are paid for by the taxpayers. But compared to traditional Medicare, the Medicare Advantage plans have four problems:
- They incur costs for profits, advertising expenses, and higher executive compensation. The only way a for-profit company can make money in an inherently unprofitable activity is to add fees to cover these extra costs.
- They incur additional costs because they were required for ideological reasons to offer some extra service (dental care or eye exams, for example) to create the illusion that the private sector could do something that traditional Medicare cannot (hence the word "Advantage" in the name).
- They have created their own networks, which has greatly reduced choices for everyone covered by Medicare. Previously, every doctor in the country had to opt either in or out of traditional Medicare.

Traditional Medicare was creating the ultimate network with most doctors getting in. Now, doctors may be in some plans but not others.
- Unlike traditional Medicare, Medicare Advantage plans have a financial incentive to deny or reduce coverage.

Since health insurance for older people is absolutely necessary and since there is no private sector alternative, Medicare is an entitlement program. Properly funded, it is simply a mechanism for Americans to make prepayments for a necessity that they would not pay be able to for any other way.

Unfortunately, two problems were built into the Medicare system at its inception. Initially, seniors who had paid very little into Medicare were insured by the contributions of younger people. But the demographic bulge of baby boomers could not easily be covered by later, smaller generations. Also, advances in medicine have dramatically driven up health care costs. Additional money is needed either from added payroll deductions or from general appropriations. Otherwise, Americans might effectively "throw the baby out with the bath water," using an aversion to taxes to eliminate the only way the overwhelming majority of people can have medical insurance late in life.

Social Security

Although relatively few people have pension plans, there are private sector plans such as 401(k)s and IRAs available to allow the prepayments necessary to fund retirement income. So why do we need Social

Security? Because most people in the United States do not save enough for retirement. No matter what their good intentions are, something always comes up: unemployment, unexpected health costs, or replacing the roof. In our market economy, forces of supply and demand in the labor market ensure that most people will not be able to reliably save enough for retirement by any mechanism other than Social Security. They simply do not make enough money. For the same reason, most people cannot pay for private schools for their children. So, ironically, government provides these two entitlements (education and Social Security) because private sector market forces prevent most people from buying them in any other way.

Some of the reasons that Social Security is important are:

- Many people would have no other retirement income. The United States would be a poorer country if a large part of its population had no resources.
- Many people who do save will have too little retirement income and will need Social Security as a supplement.
- Social Security provides nonretirement benefits such as money for widows and their children, and for the disabled.
- Social Security is not dependent on investment choices or Wall Street, so it is not subject to the volatility of the financial sector.
- Social Security protects those who do have money from those who do not. A wealthy man will benefit from his friends' and relatives' Social Security. It

may keep them from showing up at his front door expecting to be taken in.
- Like Medicare, Social Security is simply a mechanism for people to make prepayments to cover the costs of an expensive necessity. A particularly important feature of Social Security is that people cannot access their money too early or make foolish decisions with it. That would leave the rest of us unprotected from them.

The fact that people live longer now than when Social Security was created in the 1930s or when Medicare was started in the 1960s makes these programs more important than ever. There is much controversy about funding these programs. If you go to the grocery store with $25 to buy $50 worth of food, you will not be able to buy enough food. Underfunding Medicare and Social Security creates the same problem.

It is interesting to note that both Medicare and Social Security are much better funded than other entitlement programs like national defense or homeland security. No other programs have a payroll deduction (FICA) like that dedicated to Medicare and Social Security. And only these programs have trust funds. Entitlement programs like the judicial system, homeland security, and national defense face potential bankruptcy every year. The solutions for their financial problems are the same as that for Medicare and Social Security: reduce costs where possible, and pay enough to fund these essential programs.

Chapter 12
Utility and the True Value of Money

Money is a medium of exchange used to facilitate trade (chapter 6). In business transactions, every twenty dollar bill is just like every other twenty dollar bill. But the value of a twenty dollar bill or any other amount of money to any given person is determined by who possesses the money.

A destitute man walking down the street spots a twenty dollar bill in the dust and eagerly grabs it. Before this, he had nothing; now he has spending power. He is free to choose how he uses this new-found money: on food, clothing, cigarettes, beer, or any of a number of things that previously were just a dream to him. This is a memorable day in his life, the day he found the twenty dollar bill.

Suppose instead that a billionaire walking down the street sees the twenty dollar bill in the dust and picks it up. He wipes the dust off the money and realizes that his hands are now dirty. He will have to go out of his way to wash his hands before he meets his friends at a fancy restaurant. So picking up the twenty dollar bill is an inconvenience. He gets no satisfaction from it, since he virtually never uses cash for anything except tipping. The kid who cleans his golf clubs will get an especially good tip this Saturday.

Economists use the word "utility" to describe the satisfaction we get from a purchase. The homeless man will experience a great deal of utility spending the twenty dollar bill he found. For him, having any money to spend is a rare and exhilarating experience. The billionaire experiences no utility from the twenty dollar bill. All it did was dirty his hands. All of his needs are already met and he routinely buys anything he wants. Indeed, he has so many possessions that he has learned late in life that virtually the only way he can get any satisfaction from money is to give it away. He enjoys the recognition (utility) that comes from having his name associated with charitable foundations, college scholarships, and endowed professorships.

Any of us can experience the thrill of zero utility that comes from acquiring a small amount of money. Pick up a penny from the ground. It is a useful act, since the penny cannot be put back into circulation until someone picks it up. But the penny confers no real buying power. It is money, but possessing it doesn't affect your actions. You are just like a billionaire with a twenty dollar bill.

Utility does not mean usefulness. A hammer or a broom has a fixed amount of usefulness, whether using it gives you any satisfaction (utility) or not. Like love, utility is no less a real concept because it cannot be precisely measured. A dehydrated man receives more satisfaction from water than from a diamond ring. A monarch needing to escape to save his life would gladly trade his kingdom for a horse.

Suppose we are forced by adverse circumstances to spend our money very carefully (chapter 2). We first buy goods and services that give us the greatest satisfaction or highest utility, and then we buy things that are not as important to us. We would buy water before food, food before clothing, and clothing before jewelry. A gold ring provides no utility to a starving or naked man.

When a person must pay for something, the true value of the purchase is determined by the utility given up by that person. A poor person paying two dollars to ride public transportation may be forgoing food or clothing. A rich man paying the two dollars forgoes nothing.

If a person has money, the likelihood that he will spend it is determined by any unmet needs or wants that he may have. In technical economic terms, on a scale of zero to one, poor people have a marginal propensity to consume (MPC) of one. That is, they will spend all (100%) of any extra money they receive. Rich people have a marginal propensity to consume (MPC) of zero (0%) or very close to zero. They have little reason to spend any extra money they receive. This concept helps us to understand why tax cuts for the wealthy simply cause them to put most of the money in the financial sector (chapter 9)—They have a zero marginal propensity to consume. Moreover, in an economic downturn, they see few economic investment opportunities.*

---

*   This analysis considers only the impact of the receipt of incremental money from tax cuts. An even greater problem is that a mal-distribution of income and wealth tends to direct more money to the financial sector. Also, few individuals make direct economic investments. These are most often done by businesses out of business funds or borrowing based on factors that have little or nothing to do with the owners' personal income taxes. However, consider the sole owner of an unincorporated business (a Schedule C on the tax return). Suppose in June she projects that her income for the year will be $300,000. But she sees a potentially lucrative opportunity to open an additional location at a cost of $100,000, all of which will be expensed. Ironically, *higher* marginal rates of taxation will provide an extra incentive to make this economic investment since they will produce greater tax savings for the current year. It is easy to see how the high marginal tax rates (70% to 90%) during the 1950s and 1960s spurred economic investment.

By contrast, money put into the hands of poor or middle-class people is more likely to be spent. Poor people have an MPC of one and middle-class people have an MPC close to one. These people will spend money quickly and this consumption will accrue to the benefit of numerous businesses. It will sustain and increase activity in the real economy, spurring employment and real economic investment.

Because of this, it is easy to understand why cutting taxes fails as an economic stimulus plan. In our progressive tax system, higher-income people are the main beneficiaries of tax cuts but they don't spend the incremental money. Another almost comical aspect of using tax cuts as an "economic stimulus" is that the very act of cutting taxes makes it more difficult to pay off the extra debt that results from cutting taxes.

Our MPC discussion invites us to take a new view of retirees. Properly funded (!), older people are ideal economic citizens. Most will spend all the income they receive (their MPC is one) while drawing down retirement savings. They may spend more than they get in income. These older Americans help create jobs in the economy, typically without seeking jobs themselves. By adequately funding Medicare and Social Security, the nation contributes to higher employment and greater prosperity. As the baby boomers began to die ("the Great Die-Off"), the nation could find itself with reduced economic activity. Only a higher birth rate or increased immigration could compensate for this.

Chapter 13
Taxation and the Two Welfare States

Americans have been asked to contribute to their country in many ways. By far the greatest sacrifices they have made for the United States have been in the form of military service. Over the years, both volunteers and draftees have fought and died or suffered serious injuries for their country. But most contributions that Americans are asked to make take the form of taxation of some kind. While this is a trivial sacrifice compared to military service, taxation is a source of considerable controversy in the United States. This seems particularly odd given the dramatic increase in demand by citizens for government services, especially in recent years. These services include the expenses for the war on terrorism, such as homeland security and the war in Afghanistan, numerous natural disasters (hurricanes, floods, tornadoes, snowstorms, forest fires), the demands of an aging population, economic relief for people and businesses following the collapse of the financial markets in 2008, and various optional activities such as the war in Iraq, the creation of Medicare Part D, and the injection of private insurance company plans into the Medicare system (chapter 11).

While no one likes paying taxes, the resistance to taxation has been out of proportion to the sacrifice required. In fact, there has been a great movement toward cutting taxes even as the need for revenue for essential services has grown. So, reduced taxation combined with American demands for increased services, particularly since the 9/11 terrorist attacks, has greatly increased the national debt. This has severely limited the country's spending flexibility.

We noted in part I that most people must have jobs to provide for themselves and they largely have no control over the existence of those jobs. They are dependent on a functional society. This requires that their government provides necessities that they cannot provide for themselves, and all of these necessities cost money. People have a personal interest in a financially sound government with adequate resources.

Sources of Federal Revenue

Business taxes, personal income taxes, and the estate tax together make up the bulk of federal government revenue. Businesses pay taxes on profits and can, in some cases, use losses in some years to offset profits in other years. Personal income taxes are paid by higher-income Americans, a little over one-half of the population. Estate taxes are paid by the estates of those deceased individuals who leave considerable assets when they die.

Those who pay personal income taxes are subject to a progressive tax system in which they must pay taxes at higher rates on incremental income. This progressive system exists for three reasons:

- Taxes can only be gotten from those with money to pay them. Lower-income people pay nothing while higher-income people pay something.
- This system tends to require people to pay taxes in proportion to how much they benefit economically

by living and earning in the United States. Taxes can be viewed as an assessment for the economic privileges the country offers.

- While progressive tax rates require progressive monetary payments, they actually assess regressive payments in utility (chapter 12). The last $10,000 in taxes on a $1 million income requires no sacrifice in satisfaction. The only $100 in taxes that is paid on a $12,000 income may cause considerable loss of satisfaction.

There is much talk of tax simplification. This would reduce much of the work we now do to complete income tax forms. But one concern is that this change would provide a net reduction in tax revenue thus aggravating the nation's financial problems. Too often, talk of tax simplification is just a smoke screen obscuring the need to make hard choices. Rearranging the deck chairs on the *Titanic* would not have kept the iceberg from hitting it.

Some wealthy people have declared an unwillingness to pay taxes to their country even after they are dead. Certainly dead people should be provided an opportunity in a court of law to describe the loss of satisfaction imposed on them in their grave by the estate tax. Neither they nor their testimony are likely to survive cross-examination.

Inheritance taxes are typically paid by the estate, not the heirs. An exception would be inherited assets such as 401(k) or IRA plans on which taxes have been deferred. The amount of inheritance is what remains of the deceased's estate after all taxes are paid.

Welfare State vs. Welfare Society

It has been said that "great inheritance is like a lifetime supply of food stamps."* Human behavior is distorted by the assured receipt of unearned income, whether from public or private sources. In *Losing Ground*, social scientist Charles Murray's seminal 1984 study of public welfare programs; it was shown that people would make choices in life that enabled them to stay on welfare even if it meant refraining from marriage or forgoing job opportunities.** It is revealing to compare the welfare state Murray studied to the welfare society created by great inheritance.

The welfare state may produce a lack of productivity by poor people due to dependency on assured income. This is also a potential problem for wealthy people in a welfare society where trust funds and inherited wealth can stifle initiative as easily as they can provide resources for achievement. There are differences between the two forms of welfare. Sometimes, people in the welfare state are met with a presumption of incompetence, though many of them manage to improve themselves despite their slim resources. But in welfare society, there is often a presumption of competence, so opportunities may open up without regard to merit.

Many people in welfare society use their good

---

*   This quote has been attributed to Warren Buffett.
** Murray also criticizes proponents of social programs for claiming that the programs would be corrective of underlying problems. But, to cite one example, there is nothing about providing food via food stamps to prevent hunger that addresses the causes of the recipients' problems. Yet it is still a good thing to help hungry people.

fortune to fund the education necessary for professional achievement or to create business enterprises. Others will give away the money that they easily obtained. Or perhaps they will offer the world their consumption, if not their production. A possible danger is that great wealth can open a door to high political office despite lack of merit.

The creation of fortunes, not the maintenance of wealth, is what benefits the nation. Since a welfare mentality distorts behavior, simply having money may create an undue emphasis on protecting it in the financial sector for future generations, rather than using it for consumption or economic investment (chapter 9). And certainly nobody, whether born poor or rich, should be deprived of the opportunity to work, be productive, create wealth, and benefit the country.

Chapter 14
Government Efficiency and Regulation

Local television newscasts regularly feature stories of alleged government inefficiency. They disclose purchases of equipment that is never used, lack of needed equipment, too many people on a project, or too few people available to please the public. There are very few reports of comparable private sector inefficiency. But how could there be? Everything in government is public information, and any attempt to hide anything simply produces more intense scrutiny. By contrast, businesses do not air their dirty laundry. Wasteful activities, and even dangerous practices, are typically not disclosed to shareholders or even to the board of directors. They become public information only if there is a death, injury, or criminal activity. Even if the private sector had many times the number of waste-per-employee incidents that are reported in government, the general public would have no way of knowing it.

Businesses, non-profit organizations, and government all draw their employees from the same population. Often, people working in all three sectors of society live in the same neighborhood. School teachers and policemen live next to computer specialists and retail clerks, and across the street from ministers and social workers. There is no reason that one neighbor should be a better worker than another.

Profit-seeking behavior is expected among business people but is frowned upon among government, church, or charity workers. The latter are held to a higher standard. In fact, waste or corruption in the public sector typically has one of two causes:

- Employees engaging in activities for their personal benefit, perhaps wasting time on the job or stealing supplies.
- Overcharges to government by private-sector firms seeking excess profits at taxpayer expense. Defense contracts for unnecessary equipment and $10 hammers billed at $100 are typical examples. Dollar for dollar, extra profits from private sector "initiative" equal government waste in these cases.

Diseconomies of Large Scale

One difficulty of managing a large organization is that "the right hand does not know what the left hand is doing." There are a lot of things being done by many people, often at different locations. Economists call this a diseconomy of large scale. Any large organization can suffer from this problem. Much depends on the quality of managers and employees. It is not possible to draw any general conclusion that retail clerks, auto mechanics, and oil company executives are inherently more efficient than policemen, school teachers, and researchers at the Center for Disease Control.

People vocally oppose government inefficiency unless they personally benefit from it. The military built large numbers of installations all over the United States during World War II. These facilities provided jobs and spending in many communities. But long after the end of the war, cities and states across the country have fiercely opposed closing these bases, no matter how useless the facilities are. Earmarks attached to the national budget have been used to fund local projects without congressional debate. These projects are locally popular among people in the recipient states, many of whom complain about government inefficiency. So-called red-light cameras efficiently provide irrefutable evidence of drivers running stoplights. The use of these cameras allows policemen to concentrate on more serious crimes while the cameras generate revenue for cash-strapped cities. But people oppose this form of government efficiency because it might be used against them.

In assessing government efficiency, it is important to note that often the most complex activities of society are handled by the public sector. The proper functions of government fall into three categories:

- Services too important to entrust to the private sector, such as national defense, homeland security, safety and health regulation, police and fire protection, and public health.
- Desirable services which are inherently unprofitable, including public education and cheap mail delivery.
- Accumulating money via taxation or payroll deduction to pay for important personal and public needs that individuals cannot or will not reliably buy for themselves. These include Medicare, Social Security and public infrastructure.

Non-profit organizations need only deal with promoting religious doctrine or on focused charitable works. Compared to government, businesses are "one-trick ponies" whose ultimate goal is profit maximization or high return on investment. Chief executives in the private sector do not usually have to deal with uncooperative opposition parties, street protests, election campaigns, and a majority of customers who persistently won't pay for the products they receive.

Government Regulation

Regulation is among the government services too important to entrust to the private sector. In many circumstances in a market economy, inadequate regulation creates an opportunity for exploitation by profit-seekers. This exploitation may take many forms:

- Increasing profits by cutting costs on worker safety or on quality control of food products. Often the opponents of regulation also oppose judicial remedies (lawsuits) seeking punitive damages that would discourage negligent behavior.
- Manipulation of markets to increase profits. Inadequate regulation of electricity markets allowed "movements" of energy on paper for the sole purpose of creating price mark ups.
- Sales of phony financial products to unsuspecting investors. If people believe that government is the problem and not the solution, why should investors demand regulation of their financial advisors? In the recent past, some people just wanted to invest their money with Bernie Madoff and make a high return every year regardless of how the markets performed.
- Predatory loans to unsophisticated borrowers. Many people in the general public are not familiar with the dangers of excessive interest rates, fees, and penalties.

Inadequate regulation in the financial sector is particularly dangerous to ordinary consumers. In the real economy, it takes a certain amount of effort to make a defective baby crib, contaminated food, or an unsafe automobile. But it only takes a few keystrokes at a computer to create a financial document that can cause great harm.

No one understands the need to regulate human activity better than private sector businesses. They recognize the need to monitor their customers, employees, and vendors with security cameras, ID confirmations, audits, and numerous other important—and sometimes intrusive—safeguards. Problems like shoplifting, employee theft, robbery, and embezzlement will not solve themselves. Society cannot rely on self-regulation. Bank robbers are just self-regulated bank customers who naturally prefer withdrawals to deposits.

Recognizing the potential for problems and preventing their occurrence are signs of maturity in both people and society. A child will run into the street and risk getting hit by a car. An adult will look both ways first. In every area of activity, people routinely anticipate possible problems and prevent them from occurring. Physical exams and dental check-ups can save us from pain and suffering. Early detection may even allow cancer to be cured. Preventive maintenance on a car may keep it from being stuck on the side of the road.

It defies both common sense and experience to believe that alone of all areas of human activity, the economy requires no awareness or prevention of future problems. The fact that our market economy is based on the assumption that people will seek personal gain, perhaps at other people's expense, provides further notice of the need for regulation.

Those who advocate an economic system unfettered by government commit the Fallacy of Composition (chapter 5). The fact that most of the time unregulated activity serves us well, does not mean that regulation is never desirable. A swimming pool analogy is instructive. Most of the time, the swimmers happily go about their activities without the need for any intrusive authority. The lifeguard seems to be there only to improve his tan and to talk to pretty girls. But when some swimmer is in distress, no one is more important than the lifeguard. And it is often forgotten that his insistence that the facility's rules be obeyed (regulation) can prevent many serious problems.

Government will always be involved in the economic system. Ideally, it will provide regulations that prevent problems from occurring. Otherwise, it will be called on after problems have occurred to clean up the mess at taxpayers' expense. Mature business people will work with elected officials to create reasonable regulations that not only protect the public, but also protect whole industries from the actions or negligence of a few irresponsible businesses.

Chapter 15
The Business Cycle, the Great Depression, and Unemployment

Fluctuations in output in the national economy may have many causes. An economic upturn might occur if new products come on the market. These could offer widespread increases in production, consumption, and employment. Pent-up demand after a period of low economic activity can spur people to start making major purchases, such as cars and appliances. People feel more optimistic and free to spend money if they see a strong economy.

A downturn in national output may occur if people become saturated with debt after much spending, or feel less free to spend because the value of their homes or financial investments has declined. Perhaps jobs have gone overseas, raising unemployment. People will reduce spending if they sense a stagnating economy.

Economists refer to these fluctuations in output as the business cycle. Although the word "cycle" suggests some regularity, these changes in economic activity often occur unpredictably. They might even be caused by external variables such as steeply higher prices for imported oil.

Upturns, or booms, in the business cycle produce higher prices (inflation) due to increased demand. Businesses always have an incentive to increase prices. If it is possible to make a fair profit selling something for ten dollars, wouldn't it be nice to sell it for eleven? The extra dollar may be pure profit. Of course, competition constrains price increases, but in an economic boom, customers are optimistic and have more money, and so may be less resistant to paying more. An economic boom is characterized by higher output, higher prices, and lower unemployment. Interest rates may be higher due to greater demand by borrowers and the need for lenders to cover higher inflation.

The Federal Reserve System

An economic downturn, or recession, is characterized by lower prices due to less demand, by lower output, and by higher unemployment. Interest rates will be lower due to less demand by borrowers and lower inflation. In both downturns and booms in the economy, the Federal Reserve System will act to keep things from getting out of hand.

The Fed, as it is sometimes called, was created by the Federal Reserve Act of 1913.[1] Broadly speaking, it has two functions. One is to help handle everyday banking activities, such as check clearing or loans to commercial banks. It thus serves as a "banker's bank" to its member financial institutions. These activities are conducted by the twelve Federal Reserve Banks around the country.

The other function of the Fed is to maintain financial stability in the economy by preventing either excessive inflation in an economic expansion or too little output and too high unemployment in a recession. The Fed will routinely raise interest rates in a normal boom to suppress inflation. It will routinely reduce interest rates in a normal downturn to spur business activity. But what are "normal" variations in the business cycle?

To begin to define "normal" fluctuations in the

business cycle, we will restrict our discussion to changes that are entirely or predominantly due to factors in the domestic economy.* It is much more difficult for the Fed through its monetary policy or the US government through its spending (or fiscal) policy to handle variables external to the domestic economy, such as world wars or trade embargos. Sudden events that are destructive to the economy are often called "shocks" to the system.

We will define a normal variation in the business cycle to be one that is due to domestic causes and that can be corrected by Federal Reserve policy. Thus a normal boom, or a normal recession, is one that is alleviated by routine Federal Reserve actions, such as changing interest rates or forcing member commercial banks to buy or sell US Treasury securities. Since its creation, the Federal Reserve System has suppressed fluctuations in economic activity many times, often without the general public even being aware of its actions.

The Great Depression

The Great Depression was an example of an abnormal variation in the business cycle. There is considerable debate about its causes,[2] but it is generally agreed

---

*   In defining normal vs. abnormal changes in the business cycle, we restrict our definitions to changes due to domestic causes because it is not possible to generalize the economic effects of the wide variety of global forces that might interrupt the domestic economy. The effects of worldwide nuclear war, a global plague, or a huge volcanic eruption creating a cloud of dust across the planet blocking out sunlight are not easily modeled. These extreme exogenous variables are just bad news. The impact of the 1973 and 1979 oil embargos is discussed in chapter 17.

that many factors combined to produce the massive downturn in economic activity and the dramatic increase in unemployment from the late 1920s to the beginning of World War II. The Great Depression was a world-wide phenomenon affecting most developed nations.

Americans tend to think of the 1920s as a period of general prosperity, which they call the "Roaring Twenties." Certainly, the unregulated stock market was booming and there was considerable manufacturing production across the country, particularly in the East and the Midwest. But the United States was still mainly an agrarian society, with most people living on farms or ranches or in small towns tied to agricultural production. And after World War I ended, farmers who had borrowed money to expand to help supply Europe found themselves in considerable debt just as the prices of agricultural products declined.

Then, two major natural disasters created calamities that affected millions of Americans. The Great Mississippi River Flood of 1927 destroyed lives, property, and commerce in the heart of the nation.** This disaster had such a profound effect on the nation's economy that for the first time in American history, there was widespread demand for federal government intervention for a problem other than national defense. In the early 1930s, the Dust Bowl in Oklahoma, Texas, and Kansas, caused many farmers to abandon their properties and head west, flooding labor markets and communities with desperate people willing to work cheaply.

** John M. Barry, *Rising Tide* (New York: Simon & Schuster, 1997) gives an excellent history of this important event.

The Business Cycle, the Great Depression, and Unemployment

The collapse of the stock market in 1929 combined with other problems to send the economy into a downward spiral, resulting in greatly reduced output and very high unemployment. As we noted in chapter 2, a "negative multiplier effect" occurs when unemployment and lack of consumption eliminate previously existing spending patterns, causing an economic implosion. The Great Depression was such a steep downturn that Federal Reserve policy was ineffective and there is no mechanism in a market economy to reverse a very steep downward trend. In fact, by inadvertent applications of the Fallacy of Composition (chapter 5), business people will act in their own self-interest to reduce their costs in the face of decreased demand. All of their actions, such as reducing the number of their employees, keeping smaller inventories, and closing locations, will make matters worse.

The only option was intervention by the federal government. Relief efforts after the 1927 Mississippi River flood had set precedence for this. So, immediately upon taking office in 1933, President Franklin Roosevelt created numerous programs designed to offer injections of federal money into the economy to create jobs and spur economic activity. These programs were controversial. People questioned both their effectiveness and the danger posed by the national debt they created. Roosevelt decreased spending in 1937, but the economy got worse as a result. This "depression within a depression" suggested that government deficit spending to alleviate a steep economic downturn was effective.

Using net injections (government expenditures

exceeding government revenues) into the economy to increase economic activity is often referred to as Keynesian economic policy, after the famous British economist John Maynard Keynes (1883--1946).[3] The Great Depression was finally, and emphatically, ended by the largest application of Keynesian economics imaginable: World War II. In the war, massive amounts of government deficit spending funded wartime activities that dramatically reduced unemployment to about one percent. An important reason for the success of this war policy was that it was supported by nearly every American. Economic policy designed to win the war also turned the economy around.

As with any form of deferred payment (chapter 11), the government debt created by deficit spending must be paid off in the future. High rates of taxation during and after the war combined with increased post-war economic activity to make this possible. Unfortunately, in later years, elected officials and voters too often succumbed to the temptation to use government deficit spending to spur the economy without accepting the responsibility of debt repayment. In government, just as in business and personal matters, the only thing wrong with debt is not paying it off.

Our analysis of the business cycle indicated that output could fluctuate for many reasons, possibly producing economic instability. People have always sought "natural" stabilizing mechanisms that would assure a smoothly functioning, prosperous economy without the need for government intervention. One such mechanism was called Say's Law, or the law of markets, after Jean-Baptiste Say (1767-1832).[4] Say's thesis was that production automatically generates the purchasing power required for consumption. The acts of paying workers, suppliers, managers, and owners would, in the aggregate, inject just the right amount of money into the economy to fund the purchases of the goods and services produced. However, Say's Law was refuted by the fact that the decisions of money recipients did not clear the market of available products for sale. Some people might save (i.e., not spend) their money or might choose to buy imports.

There might be "leakage" in an economic system if money escapes the system. People in the United States can send money outside the country by buying imports, either of products in short supply, such as oil, or of low-cost products made by cheap labor elsewhere. Money may be held in savings temporarily. It is even possible that money on a massive scale could be removed for indefinite periods of time from the real economy. This money could be put into the financial sector in order to make profits either owning, insuring, lending for, or betting on or against activities inside the real economy (chapter 9). Advanced countries have never been further removed from the neat balance of production and consumption suggested by Jean-Baptiste Say.

One term used in discussing business cycles needs to be clarified because it is often a source of confusion. When economists declare that a recession is over, people often disagree since they may still observe economic problems, including high unemployment. In general terms, economists define "recession" as a period of declining output. To them, the recession ends when the decline in output stops. Of course, at that point, output is still down, and this is what the general public notices. For many people, the misery of unemployment continues after what economists call the end of the recession. Like many other words in the dictionary, the word "recession" can have multiple meanings. An alternative definition of recession might be a low level of economic activity accompanied by high unemployment.

Unfortunately, high unemployment may linger even as output begins to increase after a recession. The lack of job recovery, or the "stickiness" in unemployment, has several causes:

- The long-term tendency in human economic development to produce more output with fewer people (chapter 1). This process is accelerated in modern times by dramatically improved technology, which often makes it cheaper to use machines and technology instead of people.
- The high proportion of people making luxury goods, purchases that can be deferred indefinitely (chapter 2).
- The movement of jobs overseas to countries with cheaper labor (chapter 3).
- The previously mentioned forms of leakage, particularly into the financial sector, which may make less money available for consumption and jobs in the real economy.
- The worst-case scenario, in which a country has created so many problems for itself that it may face a long-term decline in economic prosperity. These problems include: ever-increasing national

debt; neglecting investments that are necessary to be competitive, such as in education and public infrastructure; not preparing for predictable problems, such as an aging population or natural disasters; inadequate regulation that allows destructive economic activity, particularly in the financial sector; and leakage to the financial sector due to uneven income distribution aggravated by tax cuts for the wealthy.

A high unemployment rate measures the degree of misery in a country, since people need to work in order to provide themselves with necessities. But a high rate of unemployment could also suggest that a country's labor is uncompetitive (low-skilled or over-priced), or that there is low demand for the country's output, or even that the country's economy is efficient (i.e., it can produce more with fewer people). In a given country in the competitive, global economy, there is no reason to believe that there are jobs available for everybody who needs a job.

Part III
American Economic History to 1981

As a graduate student and teaching assistant in the early 1970s, I frequently found myself wading through throngs of undergraduates in the halls of the mathematics department. The baby boomers were filling up the nation's colleges and universities. One day, I noticed a young man with no legs maneuvering through the crowd in a wheelchair. His face looked familiar, but how could it? I didn't know anybody without legs. A story about him in the school newspaper revealed that he had been an undergraduate student with me in the 1960s and had lost his legs in Vietnam.

In the late 1970s, a schoolteacher in the Midwest reported that his family's propane bill in the winter was nearly half his take home pay. They would pay all year for the expensive fuel needed to heat their rural home. The OPEC oil embargo had dramatically driven up the price of energy and everything else.

Meanwhile, many communities in the so-called "oil patch" states like Texas, Louisiana, and Oklahoma prospered because of high oil and natural gas prices. For some people, personal wealth and arrogance increased in equal measure. Their opinion of the impact of higher prices elsewhere in the United States—"let the bastards freeze in the dark"—earned the oil industry no friends. But the oil industry's resentment of government interference in the "free market" in the 1970s gave way to pleas for government tax breaks in the mid-80s when oil prices collapsed.

For just about everybody in the United States, there was something not to like in the 1970s and it wasn't just strange clothing and bad haircuts. The American Dream defined so neatly by the nation's prosperity in the 1950s and 1960s seemed somehow less attainable. But what happened? Was the rest of the world suddenly turning against the United States, or was there some internal enemy undermining our economic system? A review of American economic history may provide some answers.

Chapter 16
The Early Years and the Age of Delusion

No other country has achieved the economic success and wealth of the United States. Starting even before the American Revolution, frontiersmen discovered a huge land with abundant resources. They were followed by settlers who pushed the frontier from east to west as they built farms, ranches, and cities. By the time historian Frederick Jackson Turner (1861-1932) presented his famous paper "The Significance of the Frontier in American History" at the 1883 Chicago World's Fair, the frontier had disappeared. Turner's paper emphasized that the "expansion westward with its new opportunities" produced a "perennial rebirth."[1] The frontier encouraged optimism. There were always new possibilities over the next hill.

The beginning of the Industrial Revolution preceded the end of the frontier period. The railroads in the eastern United States were connected to the West when, in 1869, the Transcontinental Railroad was completed.[2] Now, the power of machines could be combined with American hard work and ingenuity to exploit the nation's vast natural resources.

The American Business Model (chapter 3) is distinctive because all of the factors necessary for economic success (natural resources, cheap labor, skilled labor, creativity, management skills, financial resources, and stable government) are contained in one domestic package. It is virtually impossible for any other country to duplicate this model. The political development of the United States is as unique as its economic development and may be as difficult to export. The American character has been determined largely by this self-contained economic system.

America's involvement in World War I was a decisive factor in the Allied victory and erased any doubts about the country's status as an important world power. Unlike European combatants, the United States was unscathed by physical destruction. Moreover, it was a creditor, not a debtor, in the inter-war squabbling over reparations and loans. Like other developed countries, the United States suffered during the Great Depression, a gigantic economic downturn emphatically ended by World War II. Except for Pearl Harbor, the country largely avoided physical destruction in that war as well. Meanwhile, Japan and Germany, as well as America's allies, were faced with the daunting task of reconstruction.

In the decades after World War II, the Unites States' economy experienced a dramatic expansion due to pent-up demand for consumer products. This was accelerated by the births of the "baby boomers." The roughly eighty million children born from 1946 to 1964 would have a great impact on the American economy at every stage of their lives. Nothing was more likely to encourage discretionary spending than small children. They would require the construction of everything from maternity wards to schools to recreation facilities.

Doting parents and grandparents lavished the boomers with toys, clothes, and trips to amusement parks. Growing families moved into ever-expanding suburbs. This greatly increased the use of the automobile. The construction of the Interstate Highway System was authorized in 1956 and completed over the next thirty-five years.[3] It allowed Americans to scurry about the country on vacations and business trips, and it prompted the construction of motels, restaurants, gas stations, and tourist attractions.

The American economic engine was hitting on all cylinders. There were a few wobbles in the economy— the occasional short periods of slightly inflationary expansion or contractionary recession—but the US economy would grow steadily after World War II. Every type of expenditure, whether necessary or discretionary, called forth increased production and created jobs. A potential problem was the entry of vast numbers of baby boomers into the workforce. The oldest turned eighteen in 1964. But the diversion of large numbers of boomers to colleges and universities made higher education a growth industry and made the United States the best-educated nation on earth.

Everyone in the world wanted American cars, clothes, and gadgets. The material wealth and abundant leisure time enjoyed by many in the United States were the envy of those in countries with undeveloped economies or economies still recovering from the war. It seemed to Americans that most people in the world woke up every morning trying to find ways to increase American prosperity, either by buying its products or by selling it cheap raw materials. The dollar was the world's strongest currency and that allowed the United States to easily finance both foreign aid and foreign military interventions. The twentieth century was unequivocally the American Century and the decades after World War II were the peak period of America's economic dominance.

The country's free-market system was so successful that Americans recommended it to other nations. Indeed, it forms the basis of the Global Business Model (chapter 3) now used by advanced economies all over the world. However, one secret ingredient in America's achievements could not be duplicated by other nations. Throughout the post-war boom, a huge contributing factor to the country's prosperity was not recognized: the United States had no competition!

After World War II, America's allies such as Great Britain and France, as well as the former Axis powers Germany and Japan, had to rebuild their economies. Communist countries such as the Soviet Union had to deal with post-war reconstruction and were burdened by the inefficiencies of their peculiar economic systems. Countries like South Korea, China, and Brazil had not yet become significant players in the global economy. America's post-war history may only indicate how a free-market economy can thrive absent any external competition. Certainly the United States had formidable productive capacity. However, America was untested in a world in which many other nations were increasingly capable of using cheap labor, natural resources, and advanced technology to make competitive products.

The post-World War II period forms the economic reference point for Americans who either grew up then or who were influenced by their elders who lived in that era. Everything seemed to come easily. There is nothing like a lack of external competition to enable domestic economic success in a resource-rich country with a growing population. But in the modern world, China, India, South Korea, Brazil, Russia, Germany, France, Japan, the United Kingdom, and numerous other countries working for their own interests are not likely to go away any time soon.

America's opinion of its place in the economic world is completely distorted by its experiences in, and constant references to, this anomalous period of post-war prosperity during which the United States was blessed by an economic system unfettered by external competition. For a period of about a quarter of a century, a nation was born on third base and thought it had hit a triple. Given the complexities and problems of the modern world, the United States cannot afford to base its economic and political policies on lingering memories of what now must be referred to as the Age of Delusion.

Chapter 17
The 1970s: A Period of Transition

The 1970s provided a jolt to both the American psyche and the US economy. The decade started ominously with the stock market crash of 1970. This brought an end to the so-called "go-go years" of unrestrained stock speculation.[1] Even Texas billionaire Ross Perot lost $450 million during this period. The downturn ended the practice of creating unmanageable conglomerates of companies as a vehicle for pumping up stock prices. The Watergate scandal (1972–1974) ended Richard Nixon's presidency and was followed by the loss of the Vietnam War. The last American soldier left Saigon on April 30, 1975.

The stock market crash, Watergate, and the Vietnam War were self-inflicted wounds, but the 1973 Arab oil embargo was something else entirely. A bunch of third-world oil-exporting countries brought the US economy to its knees. Operating as OPEC (the Organization of the Petroleum Exporting Countries), this cartel interfered with the functions of crude oil markets by colluding to reduce exports and artificially drive up prices. While the embargo produced higher fuel prices and lines at gas stations, the furor over Watergate initially got far more attention. People also paid little attention to Nixon's anti-inflation program called WIN, for Whip Inflation Now.

Beginning with this embargo, the American economy would no longer be viewed as a simple, self-contained system. The United States was the world's largest importer of crude oil, and its price and availability would henceforth be a subject of concern. But how did higher oil prices have such a great impact on the United States and what ended the resulting downturn in the country's economy?

During and immediately after World War II, America was a major oil exporter. The giant East Texas Oil Field produced over 542 million barrels of oil from 1942 to 1945, providing the United States and its allies with abundant fuel.[2] This gave them a significant advantage over Germany and Japan, both of which struggled to obtain adequate oil supplies. After the war, cheap oil fueled the booming US economy. But depleting fields and economic expansion eventually made the country an oil importer.

The OPEC embargo quickly increased crude oil prices from $3.29 per barrel in 1972 to $11.58 per barrel in 1974, and by 1980, they approached $40 per barrel.[3] This doesn't seem like much now, but it represents a 1,100 percent price increase in less than nine years for an essential commodity. These higher oil prices also brought increased prices for substitute fuels such as natural gas and coal. Higher prices at the gas pump were accompanied by higher utility costs. These were direct price increases for consumers. But everybody who used energy—manufacturers, retailers, distributors, and service providers—had higher fuel costs and it was easy for businesses to pass on the higher costs to consumers because all of their competitors were doing so. It seemed like the price of everything went up significantly from 1973 to 1982. People paid more for ice cream because of the OPEC oil embargo.

Higher oil prices increased inflation which prompted the Federal Reserve System to raise interest rates. Also, lenders paid careful attention to the rate of inflation when deciding what interest rates to charge borrowers. No one would offer a loan at a low interest rate in an era of high inflation since the real value of the money repaid would be less than the value of the money loaned.

High inflation also meant that overall purchases and output were reduced since more money was being spent on the energy component of products. This is what economists call an "income effect": more money spent on one thing leaves less money to buy something else. Finally, the reduction in output increased unemployment. This unusual combination of economic problems (high inflation, high interest rates, reduced national output, and high unemployment) were caused by the 1973 oil embargo and came to be called "stagflation." This was not a typical economic downturn since it was caused by forces external to the domestic economy (chapter 15).

During this period of time, many employees asked for and received a "cost of living adjustment" (COLA) to offset the inflation they were encountering. But this was an example of the Fallacy of Composition (chapter 5). COLAs just caused prices to go up even more, since the cost of labor is the only factor that has a greater impact on inflation than the cost of energy. The nation's problems grew even worse in 1979 with a second OPEC oil embargo.

It was a truly miserable time for Americans. High interest rates made it difficult for both consumers and businesses to finance purchases. Sales of big-ticket items like houses and cars particularly suffered and many people were out of work. Fortunately, the OPEC cartel's plan to interfere with crude oil markets and increase oil prices carried within it the seeds of its own destruction.

Higher energy costs naturally induced conservation and fuel savings. People adjusted their thermostats. They used their cars less often. Some joined car pools or used public transportation. Businesses especially had an incentive to cut costs since many were huge consumers of energy. Government-mandated reduced speed limits also helped. The nation needed to stem the massive outflow of money paid for oil imports. At the same time, higher energy prices motivated oil exploration companies all over the world to expand their search for hydrocarbons. Often it takes years for these projects to go through the stages of exploration, wildcat drilling, development drilling, and pipeline construction necessary for ultimate product delivery.

By 1982, a combination of reduced demand and increased supply of energy caused oil prices to flatten and they steadily collapsed to under $10 per barrel in 1986. The market economy had worked to effectively "undo" the interference in the marketplace caused by OPEC, but the American people had experienced a brutal introduction to external economic forces that did not work to their advantage.

A more subtle phenomenon of the 1970s was the emergence of Japan as an economic power. The Japanese would rebuild after World War II and create the second largest economy in the world. If a small, highly-populated nation with limited resources could become both a major exporter to, and competitor of, the United States, what might other, larger countries achieve if they entered the global economy? A more immediate question was this: would Americans resist threats posed by external restrictions on essential raw materials and increased foreign competition, or would they merely wallow in nostalgia for the Age of Delusion?

Chapter 18
The Age of Denial

It seems somehow fitting that the 1970s would end with the Iranian hostage crisis.[1] On November 4, 1979, students and militants in support of the Iranian revolution took over the US Embassy in Tehran. They held fifty-three Americans captive for 444 days. In the larger scheme of world history, this was a non-event. Any nation's embassy in a hostile country could be taken over by a large mob if the host country didn't provide adequate security. But this crisis became a big issue because it occurred during the 1980 presidential election. A rescue attempt in April, 1980, was aborted due to mechanical problems with several helicopters. Then, eight servicemen were killed and several injured in a refueling accident when the helicopters were preparing to leave.

This appeared to be just another example of America's helplessness. After all, if a third-world country like North Vietnam could defeat the American military, if a band of third-world oil exporters could cripple the US economy, and if a little country like Japan could challenge the United States economically, then why shouldn't a bunch of Iranian students affect an American presidential election? Appropriately enough, the hostages would be released on Inauguration Day, January 20, 1981.

The 1980 election would not only determine who occupied the White House for the next four years; it would decide how Americans would choose to face a changing world. The election pitted incumbent Democrat Jimmy

Carter against the Republican challenger, Ronald Reagan. Both men were former state governors but the resemblance ended there. Carter was a Georgia peanut farmer and a Navy-trained nuclear engineer. Reagan was a former Hollywood actor and television star. Carter was a problem-solver who famously wore a sweater as he turned down the thermostat in the White House to use less heat during the 1970s energy crisis. He came across as serious, even sullen, during this period of time. Reagan was personable, eloquent, and photogenic. He challenged the very notion that Americans, with their great history, should have to suffer due to the actions of lesser nations.

Carter had inherited the country's economic woes from his Republican predecessors, who had also been powerless to overcome the 1973 oil embargo. But Reagan successfully blamed Carter for the nation's problems and was elected president by a wide margin. Ultimately, the economy would recover when market forces lowered the price of oil in the mid-1980s (chapter 17). Lower energy costs would reduce inflation and allow lower interest rates. This made more money available for non-energy consumption which in turn increased the nation's productive output and reduced unemployment.

In his inaugural address, Ronald Reagan had declared that "government was not the solution, government was the problem." But the problems of the 1970s had nothing to do with government. Those problems, which included the economic downturn at the beginning of the Reagan administration, were not caused by government regulations, government inefficiency, taxation levels, or by government in any way.

President Reagan advocated the largest tax cut in American history and it was passed by a Democratic Congress in 1981. But reducing income taxes didn't end the OPEC oil embargo and, in fact, may have made Americans more resistant to conservation. For that matter, lower taxes didn't reverse the defeat in Vietnam or slow down the Japanese economy. The Reagan tax cuts seemed apropos of nothing but ideology.

For some politicians, tax cuts and deregulation would become the default fiscal policy regardless of surrounding economic reality. These politicians saw government as the enemy and blamed any departure from the prosperity of the post-World War II era on government interference in the market. Many Americans resisted the notion that external forces could negatively impact their once self-contained economy. They were reluctant to leave the Disneyland of the 1950s and 1960s. By 1981, the United States had firmly and forcefully entered the Age of Denial.

Part IV
Ideology and Conflict

Historically, economic downturns in the United States have disproportionately impacted blue-collar workers and low-level office employees with little education. This was evident after the 1973 OPEC oil embargo and even during the turmoil in the financial markets in the 1980s. But in the twenty-first century, even highly skilled, well-educated executives and professionals lost jobs.* Recessions have become an equal-opportunity experience. Everybody is affected by global competition and the long-term trend in human economic development of producing more with less people.

Since 1980, Americans have experienced armed conflicts, big swings in energy prices, and political bickering, as well as a severe economic downturn. During this time, the country's problems and the actions of the American government have not always been determined by objective forces such as market changes or physical assaults on the nation. Ideology—the sometimes unfounded opinions of highly fallible human beings—was often used to justify wars, and to promote certain economic and fiscal policies. We can better understand contemporary issues if we look at this era in its entirety.

---

* Barbara Ehrenreich, *Bait and Switch* (New York: Henry Holt and Company, 2005) explores the impact of job loss on higher-level, white-collar workers.

Chapter 19
Tax Cuts, Distribution, and Redistribution

In 1981, Ronald Reagan's seemingly extraneous attack on the government (it was not the solution, it was the problem) raised several fundamental questions. In a country like the United States, what does it mean to complain about the government? The people control the government through their elected representatives. If cutting taxes is desirable, is it really possible to just look at an income tax table and declare that taxes are too high? Is a 70 percent marginal tax rate too high? Is a 10 percent marginal rate too high? Since tax revenues are simply the means to pay for actions by government determined in a manner defined by the US Constitution, wouldn't democracy be undermined by an arbitrary tax reduction? After all, taxation is merely a predictable result of people's demand for government services.

Everyone wants more money, so it will always be easy to garner support for tax cuts. But the services Americans demand from their government are many and costly: defense, domestic security, public education, infrastructure, disaster relief, public health, and many others. Voters complain about government, especially at election time, but they demand things from government all the time. Most people would not even consider walking out of a store without paying for something (shoplifting), but they will routinely vote for politicians who promise them both tax cuts and government services. And everyone's individual desire to pay fewer taxes is an application of the Fallacy of Composition (chapter 5) waiting to happen.

What does it really mean to say "I don't like paying taxes"—or, more generally—that you don't "like" something? If surgery saves your life after a serious illness and then someone asks if you liked the surgery, how do you reply? Yes? But the surgery and recovery were very painful. No? But the surgery saved your life.

If certain government programs benefit other people and not you, should you vote for tax cuts in protest? If these tax reductions turn out to be so drastic that they also eliminate government services important to you and those you care about, would you blame this result on the politicians? Compromises are necessary in a country with many people having diverse needs and viewpoints. A person in an undeveloped country lacking government services would argue that having to pay taxes because you are a prosperous American is a nice problem to have. And a progressive income tax system (chapter 13) should provide assurance that if you pay a lot of taxes, then you must make a lot of money.

The net effect of government spending is to redistribute money from wealthier taxpayers to those who pay little or no tax. Poor people get the benefit of roads, bridges, national defense, and public hospitals. Is this bad? Americans can recite the deficiencies of redistributive, or socialistic, economic systems, principally their lack of financial incentives for personal initiative and creativity. But society must find some mechanisms to help the young, the old, and the unfortunate (chapter

10). And in a large country, large problems often require large solutions. Also, many prominent people have pointed to the value of altruism. For example, Jesus Christ advocated helping the less fortunate, and He has quite a following. He may, however, lack credibility among the free-market ideologues who emphasize the importance of self-interest. Perhaps His Father never taught Him about the virtues of capitalism.

Distribution vs. Redistribution

Economic systems that distribute output only as determined by market mechanisms may produce huge, even comical, levels of income and asset mal-distribution. Also, a pure market economy does not provide any public services like defense, interstate highways, or the public education needed for a prosperous society of consumers and producers. The deficiencies of free-market, or capitalistic, economic systems are remedied by redistribution through taxation and government services.

A mirror image of this phenomenon is that the deficiencies of redistributive economic systems must be corrected by the introduction of market mechanisms which encourage and reward individual initiative. Pure socialistic systems with government-controlled economies are stagnant. They must have some significant component of market-based economic activity in order to grow and prosper.

Capitalism and socialism are extremist economic ideologies. Each of them is inconsistent with people's desire for prosperity, fairness, and security in a democratic society. At best, these extremist economic systems are only reference points for discussing the relative proportion of distributive and redistributive features that a truly functional economy must have. The "optimal" economic system is a combination of private sector activities and government services that together meet the needs of the people.**

Conservatives vs. the Government

What motivated Ronald Reagan and his followers to attack government and push for income tax reduction in 1981? Some Republicans had been out of step with the American majority since the Roosevelt administration's widespread use of federal programs to aid people in the Great Depression. And more recent events in American history had just reinforced their views of the place of the federal government in American society.

** "Distribution" refers to the allocation of resources in a market economy unfettered by government. "Redistribution" refers to any forces, voluntary or involuntary, which allocate resources to those who would not otherwise receive them in a market economy. This is a more general view of the problem of resource allocation than the simplistic battle between capitalism and socialism. In *Language in Thought and Action* (San Diego: Harcourt Brace Jovanovich, 1990), S.I. Hayakawa reminds us that the choice of words matters in framing a debate. Every economy has both distributive and redistributive features. Even rigidly controlled communist systems often had black market activities that allowed market forces to work. Redistribution is rampant in the United States, and without it, we would not have public infrastructure, public schools, national defense, and many other things. Still, the word "redistribution" is often used in an inflammatory manner. A measure of the complexity of this controversy is that, historically, two leading proponents of redistribution are Jesus Christ and Karl Marx.

TAX CUTS, DISTRIBUTION, AND REDISTRIBUTION

Many conservatives saw the 1960s and 1970s as a period of instability in the United States. Anti-war protests, bra-burning women's rights activists, race riots, pot-smoking hippies, striking migrant workers, and college students taking over school administration buildings were all viewed as signs of a societal breakdown. Liberal politicians in Washington promoted the social changes that caused this unrest. And federal taxes were used to pay for an array of social programs, including the War on Poverty, food stamps, and welfare, which conservatives believed should be either left to the states or not done at all. In fact, social change in this era was overwhelmingly peaceful. The civil rights movement was patterned after the methods of non-violent civil disobedience that Mahatma Gandhi (1869–1948)[1] used to overcome British rule in India. American civil rights protestors courageously endured beatings and worse in an effort to end racial inequality. The societal changes in the 1960s and 1970s were almost uniformly beneficial to the United States. For example, before the civil rights era, the South had been socially and economically stifled for centuries. Racial integration was a necessary condition for the South's economic revival in the late twentieth century that came to be known as the New South.

But to those who placed a higher premium on peace, law and order, and unimpeded commerce, federal government actions in support of social change smacked of high-handed interference in personal life and business. Some things were better left to individual choice and the marketplace. But so many Americans supported the various social causes, it was politically necessary to attack the government in more general terms as an inefficient and expensive intrusion in people's lives.

Like many other Americans, conservatives misunderstood the nature of their country's problems in the 1970s (chapter 17). To conservatives, Richard Nixon's Watergate escapade was an attempt to protect society from radical forces, and the Vietnam War was lost by draft-card burning anti-war protestors. They claimed that America's economic downturn in that decade was due to excessive government interference in society. They believed that if people just had more personal freedom, then the combined forces of a free society and a free-market economy would produce social stability and economic prosperity.

Noted conservative economist Milton Friedman (1912–2006) promoted these ideas. In his popular book, *Free to Choose*,[2] and in his PBS documentary by the same name, Friedman introduced many people to elementary economic concepts that they were supposed to know before they proclaimed themselves free-market advocates. But what Friedman and many other economists did not address was that for the first time in its history, the United States had to deal with global economic forces that worked against it and that it could not easily control. Neither the OPEC oil embargo nor the rise of Japan as the world's second great economic power was due to a lack of personal freedom by Americans.

But who could argue with personal freedom? It was the ideal plank in any political platform. We should be able to do what we want. Who wants to submit to a military draft or a zoning ordinance or a stop sign? And to some conservatives, the doctrine of lower taxes joined the list of unalienable rights endowed by their Creator along with life, liberty, and the pursuit of happiness. Lost in all this banter was the fact that the United States was already the freest country on earth.

In 1981, Reagan began his experiment of cutting federal taxes. Proponents said that President John F. Kennedy's reduction in income taxes in the early 1960s had produced an era of economic prosperity. They did not point out that even after Kennedy's tax cut, the highest marginal tax rates were 77 percent in 1964 and 70 percent thereafter.[3] A prosperous economy could possibly allow both tax cuts and adequate government spending without creating large budget deficits. So the open question in the first year of Ronald Reagan's presidency was: would either inadequate growth or Americans' demands for government services make tax cuts unaffordable?

Chapter 20
Lessons of War

The private sector alone will not provide every service necessary to sustain a prosperous nation, so public policy decisions are important. Will adequate security, education, infrastructure, public health services, and disaster relief be available? Is taxation sufficient to pay the bills that come due for these government services, or could future generations be stuck with their parents' and grandparents' debts? Will lack of adequate financial regulation produce occasional economic shocks that set the nation back? An important concern is that sometimes ideology and pre-conceived ideas overwhelm both practical considerations and the requirements of our modern economy. An examination of another category of important decisions—whether or not to go to war—can provide insight into how our leaders determine public policy.

In World War II, the Axis powers sought global domination by conquering all the other advanced industrial nations of the world.[1] In Europe, German forces swept from France to the Soviet Union before getting bogged down in the Russian winter of 1941 while trying to take Moscow.[2] Nazi forces even spilled over into North Africa. In Asia, Japan invaded Manchuria on the Chinese mainland and took over Pacific islands all the way to the Philippines. The United States entered the war after the Japanese bombed Pearl Harbor on December 7, 1941.

Allied forces defeated Germany in North Africa in May 1943. After the June 6, 1944, D-Day landing on the coast of France, the United States and its allies pushed toward Germany. With Soviet forces advancing from the east, the Nazis were forced to surrender on May 8, 1945—Victory in Europe (V-E) Day. In the Pacific theater, American forces liberated conquered islands and advanced toward Japan itself. The fierce resistance of Japanese fighters during this "island-hopping" campaign served as a warning that any invasion of Japan would produce a long and deadly struggle for the United States. As a result, choosing to drop atomic bombs on Hiroshima and Nagasaki in August 1945 was perhaps the easiest decision in the history of warfare. World War II ended with the unconditional surrender of Japan on V-J Day, August 15, 1945.

After North Korea invaded South Korea on June 25, 1950, the United Nations formed a coalition of sixteen countries to repel the invaders.[3] Since 90 percent of the troops were Americans, this war was a reunion for many veteran soldiers who had fought together only five years earlier in World War II. The objective in Korea seemed to be the same as in the previous war: regain lost territory and defeat the enemy.

The UN coalition needed only to reclaim South Korean territory and then take over, or at least severely punish, North Korea. In September and October of 1950, UN forces entered North Korea but there was a wrinkle in the Korean War unlike anything encountered in WWII. China entered the war and, from November 1950 to January 1951, Chinese forces drove the UN coalition out of North Korea and entered the south. By July 1953, however, the United States and its UN allies regained

South Korean territory. This produced an armistice but no peace treaty was ever signed.

France occupied all or parts of Vietnam from 1856 until the French defeat at Dien Bien Phu in 1954 by the resourceful forces of communist North Vietnam.[4] The French had been weakened militarily and economically by WWII and withdrew from Vietnam. The United States stepped in to support the anti-communist government of South Vietnam, initially with military advisors and equipment. Fearful of communist expansion in Southeast Asia, American forces effectively took over the war from South Vietnam. The United States ultimately suffered 58,000 dead and many more injured, often with invisible wounds including psychological damage and chemical exposure.

The Cold War Imperative

It is difficult now to fully appreciate the obsession with defeating communism during the Cold War. Americans fly joint missions in space with Russians and buy numerous Chinese products everyday. But in the 1960s, stopping the communist menace was an ideological imperative. President Lyndon Johnson (1908–1973) used an apparent skirmish in the Tonkin Gulf in August 1964 as a pretext to dramatically expand America's involvement in the war.

The rest, as they say, is mystery. The United States attempted to apply the WWII territorial strategy, repeatedly defeating the communists in villages and hamlets and rice paddies. The Marines and the Army would take one hill only to abandon it in order to claim another hill.

The war effort was propelled more by politicians' fears of being labeled soft on communism and by notions of American invincibility on the battlefield than by any serious consideration of the difficulties of fighting a motivated enemy in its homeland.

With Korea as an analogy, Americans assumed that the objective in the war was to enforce a border between South Vietnam and North Vietnam. But on January 31, 1968, the combined forces of the army of the Republic of North Vietnam and the Viet Cong communist guerillas took advantage of the Tet holiday to attack the American and South Vietnamese armies in a coordinated effort. While these many assaults were successfully repelled, the Tet Offensive demonstrated that the enemy was in front and in back, to the right and to the left, and also right on top of, American forces in the US Embassy compound in Saigon. For Americans, there was no definition of victory in Vietnam.

If Americans believed their own rhetoric about the superiority of democracy and capitalism, then communist countries would eventually collapse under the weight of economic inefficiency and societal misery. So why send Americans half way around the world to fight and die against any country hell-bent on self-destruction? And why enter a civil war in Vietnam to aid South Vietnam, hardly a well-defined democracy with wide support? But ideology and pre-conceived ideas overwhelmed any realistic assessments of how or why to fight in Vietnam.

The US Army was not allowed to reason why, but it had to fight and die. After the war, it asked itself the obvious question, "How could a small country like Vietnam defeat the world's greatest military superpower?" Certainly, many factors worked against the United States in Vietnam. The communists were never going to leave their own country, and they knew that US forces would not stay there forever. Any American expansion of combat designed to overrun Vietnam from south to north would simply bring China into the war, as in Korea. And many American military advantages were nullified in street-to-street, house-to-house, hand-to-hand combat. It was hard to send a submarine or aircraft carrier through a Vietnamese village or call in a nuclear strike when an American platoon was engaged in a tough firefight.

The US Army created the Center for Army Lessons Learned (CALL) at Fort Leavenworth, Kansas, to study the war. It determined that Vietnam was not a territorial war like WWII but was instead a counter-insurgency war.[5] Much of the South Vietnamese population had no particular allegiance to either side. Asia is a very big and lonely place to fight, especially if neither your enemy nor your ally is well-defined. Counter-insurgency strategy required that much effort be made to insure that the native population was on the Army's side. Otherwise, it might be fighting for nothing.

Prior to the Vietnam War, the Soviet Union and China had differences in how to apply communist theory, with the Chinese claiming greater ideological purity. This Sino–Soviet split was so intense that there was speculation in the West about what would happen if war broke out on the long border between Russia and China. The

Soviet Union had great technological superiority, but China had much more manpower. Would the Soviets bomb themselves with atomic weapons to repel an invasion of twenty million Chinese? America's participation in the Vietnam War united these two communist countries in a common cause. This would destroy an advantage for the West in the Cold War regardless of the outcome in Vietnam.

Diplomacy and Limited Resource Strategy

It is important to understand the strategy used by the Soviet Union and China in this war. They provided North Vietnam with huge amounts of military equipment and consumer goods thus helping the Vietnamese communists match American resources. So with only very minimal manpower contribution—a few advisors—the Soviets and Chinese were able to help defeat their primary Cold War enemy without leaving the comforts of their homes and offices. They did not have to deal with nasty issues like death, injury, or determining the difference between allies and enemies. These communist powers effectively won the war using a "rocking chair" strategy of simply directing resources to their ally.

The United States would successfully use this "rocking chair" or diplomacy and limited resource (DLR) strategy to intervene in the Soviet–Afghan War (1979–1989). In 1978, left-wing military leaders and civilians with Soviet support overthrew the Afghan government despite widespread opposition. Many Afghans fled east to Pakistan and formed the Mujahideen, a rebel force opposing the new government. In 1979, the Soviet Union sent in troops to quell the Mujahideen fighters.[6] The Soviets' ideology required that they support communist expansion everywhere in the world.

This Soviet invasion attracted Islamist fighters from all over the Middle East. Islamism is a doctrine opposing foreign occupation in the Muslim world.[*] The Islamists opposed the Russian invasion for the same reason that Americans would oppose a Muslim army invading North America. The Islamists also oppose what they see as infidel influences on their people, such as loose sexual behavior, revealing clothing, or any religious practices they disagree with. This is very much like what evangelical preachers in the United States would warn against in their Sunday sermons. Among the Islamists fighting with the Mujahideen were the Saudi Osama bin Laden, the Egyptian doctor Ayman al-Zawahiri, and their followers. During this war, the two men would unite to form the Islamist terrorist organization al-Qaeda.

The United States also supported the Mujahideen fighters by providing them with equipment, notably shoulder-mounted, heat-seeking rockets which effectively converted Russian helicopter gunships from deadly weapons to death traps. The Soviet forces began withdrawing in 1988 and were gone by 1989. The Mujahideen finally overthrew the left-wing government in Kabul in 1992. Eventually, religious students called the Taliban, who had fled Afghanistan to go to Pakistan, returned and took over the government. The United

---

* Islamism is discussed in Lawrence Wright, *The Looming Tower* (New York: Vintage, 2006).

States had defeated the Soviet Union in an Asian war without putting "boots on the ground" or even wings in the air.

The Collapse of the Soviet Union

This war was Russia's Vietnam, and this military defeat was one of several factors that together broke up the Soviet Union.** The Cold War conflict between the United States and the Soviets was such a huge part of American history after WWII that it is worth reviewing the break-up of the USSR. The Soviet army was a brutal institution, and its reputation was not enhanced in the eyes of the Russian people by body bags coming back from Afghanistan. Also, a new generation of Russian youth liked Beatles' music and American clothes. They were not likely to accept the strict anti-Western policies of their elders. The collapse of oil prices in the 1980s (chapter 17) deprived the Soviet Union of its main source of hard currency from exports.

Mikhail Gorbachev (1931–) would be the last leader of the Soviet Union; largely because he was the first leader of the Soviet Union who did not come from the old hard-line Stalinist era communists. Gorbachev advocated "perestroika," or reforms to improve efficiency and

---

** Information on the collapse of the Soviet Union is from *World Book Encyclopedia* 11th Edition, s.v. "Soviet Union." Note that neither Ronald Reagan's tax cuts nor his defense spending caused the Soviet's loss in Afghanistan, the election of Mikhail Gorbachev, the opposition to the USSR in Soviet bloc countries such as Poland, or the decline in oil prices in the 1980s that kept the USSR from supporting its far-flung empire.

increase growth. He encouraged "glasnost," or freedom of expression. His policies weakened the iron grip of the Communist Party in the Soviet Union.

When shipyard workers in Gdansk, Poland, went on strike in 1980 for higher pay, trade unions, and political reform, there was no Russian army response as in Hungary (1956) or in Czechoslovakia (1968). The Soviet army was tied up in Afghanistan. By the time the Polish workers' Solidarity union was recognized in 1989, the Soviets were too weak to offer resistance. The Berlin Wall fell that year and by October 1991, member countries began leaving the Soviet Union.

When Iraq invaded Kuwait in 1990, the United States under President George H. W. Bush (1924–) formed a coalition of thirty-nine countries to repel the invaders.[7] Kuwait and nearby Saudi Arabia were leading sources of oil for the Western world and had to be protected. The Bush administration recognized this as a territorial war. The enemy was pushed back with a loss of as many as 100,000 Iraqi troops. A cease-fire agreement was signed on April 6, 1991.

The Gulf Coalition chose not to attempt an overthrow of the Saddam Hussein regime by invading Iraq and taking over Baghdad. This would have created a counter-insurgency war similar to Vietnam. Also, the United States and its allies would have found themselves in the middle of a prolonged civil war between the ruling Sunni Muslim population and the larger Shiite Muslim plurality.

The United States responded to the 9/11 terrorist attacks by destroying the al-Qaeda training camp in

Afghanistan in October 2001.[8] But what should be done next? Al-Qaeda was not a country. It had no territory and it had no military. It was a loose coalition of Islamist extremists from many nations that at various times had operatives in Afghanistan, Germany, Great Britain, Indonesia, Pakistan, Saudi Arabia, Spain, Sudan, the United States, and Yemen. One possibility was diplomacy and limited resource (DLR) war, focused on killing or capturing the al-Qaeda leadership. Osama bin Laden and Ayman al Zawahiri were thought to be hiding in the Afghanistan–Pakistan border region. Instead, the United States under President George W. Bush (1946–) chose a territorial war. It overthrew the Taliban government in Afghanistan with the intent of establishing a Muslim democracy. This added "nation building" to the task at hand: defeating al-Qaeda.

Another Iraq War

Before the wisdom of this strategy could be determined, the Bush administration inexplicably declared war on Iraq.[9] This was an odd decision, since the Iraqis had been severely beaten in the 1991 Gulf War, incurring significant damage both to their military and to their infrastructure. Restrictions on their oil revenues by the United Nations greatly limited the availability of resources for hostile activities. More importantly, the United States maintained continuous control over Iraqi airspace with fighter planes armed with missiles. These planes could cover Iraq 24/7 from bases in Turkey and from aircraft carriers in the Persian Gulf. They could take out anything in Iraq on short notice. This Policy of

Containment[10] carried minimal risk of life or limb to any American and cost about $1.5 billion a year, about what it would cost per week to fight the Iraq War.

Like Vietnam, the 2003 Iraq War was a triumph of ideology over reality. It was pushed by two groups of ideologues. Traditional hawkish Republicans believed that the administration of George W. Bush's father, George H.W. Bush, had blown an opportunity at the end of the Gulf War to help the Shiite opposition in Iraq overthrow Saddam Hussein. Neo-conservatives also supported this aggressive action against Iraq. The neo-conservative movement included many pro-Israeli Democrats who wanted to establish a precedent for aggressive American military action in the world in anticipation of US forces someday protecting Israel. These two groups created such a clamor for invading Iraq that most public discourse was drowned out. Threats plus accusations of unpatriotic motives or cowardice stifled any remaining dissent. Saddam Hussein was accused of harboring weapons of mass destruction. Pro-war ideologues accepted any "evidence" that supported this, no matter how unreliable. For example, an Iraqi exile named Ahmed Chalabi was a key source of information. Chalabi was intent on replacing Saddam Hussein in Iraq and was known by the US intelligence community to be deceitful. But no evidence of weapons of mass destruction was found before, during, or after the war.

The ideologues further insinuated that Saddam Hussein had participated somehow with al-Qaeda in the 9/11 terrorist attacks. This was illogical. Al-Qaeda was a coalition of Muslim terrorists. Saddam Hussein was a secular dictator who patterned his leadership style after the Russian, Joseph Stalin. Hussein cooperated with no one. Al-Qaeda had a training camp in Afghanistan. American ideologues hypothesized the existence of an al-Qaeda camp in Iraq, but Hussein would not have tolerated a group of armed Muslim militants in his country.

The invasion of Iraq, the overthrow of Saddam Hussein, the disbanding of the Iraqi army, and the destruction of civil authority effectively allowed terrorists to enter a country that had been off limits under Hussein. The terrorist group called "Al-Qaeda in Iraq" did not exist before the Iraq War. This war was not merely pointless; it was counterproductive, since it allowed the Taliban and al-Qaeda in Afghanistan time to regroup. The Afghanistan War became a counter-insurgency war. About 3,000 Americans died on 9/11. Over 4,400 Americans died in the Iraq War. This is not what people mean when they advocate beating al-Qaeda. America's volunteer military has borne the brunt of the wars in Iraq and Afghanistan while most Americans blithely went about their business. Perhaps willful denial has helped.

Territorial wars have better defined objectives than counter-insurgency wars and tend to be shorter. DLR wars have less at stake than more full-blown commitments. They minimize the damage caused by ideologically motivated actions and are a more economic use of America's resources. Americans should reflect on how easy it was to use ideology to justify going to war. It is even easier for extremists to push foolish economic policies since no apparent loss of life is involved.

Chapter 21
Reagan, Bush, and Clinton

Ronald Reagan formally declared his opposition to government in his Inauguration Day speech, and his 1981 appointment of Stanford law professor William F. Baxter[1] as head of the Anti-trust Division of the Department of Justice made that opposition tangible. Baxter adhered to the Chicago School of Economics, which believed that markets would maximize production from available resources if they were allowed to operate free of government interference. A former Baxter student, attorney Gary Reback wrote in his book *Free the Market* that the Anti-trust Division under Baxter ended a thirteen-year-old anti-trust case against IBM and dropped "cases against Mack Trucks, Mercedes Benz, General Electric, a group of hotels in Hawaii, and two manufacturers of facing bricks." It also abandoned court orders against can manufacturers, Safeway grocery, and other companies. Under Reagan, the American people would be protected by the virtues of profit-seeking businessmen operating in their own self interest.

No segment of the economy was more eager to take advantage of Reagan's laissez-faire policy than the financial sector. Investment bankers, short-sellers, and arbitrageurs were by nature opportunists, and any lack of regulation invited exploitation. There are many ways to make money in this world. Why would anyone soil their hands producing goods or services if they could make a fortune moving paper around? Financiers would have a field day in the Reagan administration.

In his *Wall Street: A Cultural History,* Steve Fraser noted that "between 1980 and 1988 the cumulative value of mergers and acquisitions, corporate takeovers, and leveraged buy-outs amounted to two-thirds of a trillion dollars." Between 1984 and 1990, a quarter of all private investment was in the finance, insurance, and real estate (FIRE) sector. And "by the mid-1980s FIRE led the pack in campaign donations and lobbying budgets."[2] Corporate raiders took over long-established companies, closed plants, laid-off employees, and changed management to produce short-term cost savings. This raised stock prices allowing quick profits. Just the threat of a takeover let corporate raiders extract tribute from management called "greenmail." Arbitrageurs like Ivan Boesky dealt in illegal inside information to do deals funded by junk-bond king Michael Milken.

In another part of the financial sector, the savings and loan (S & L) industry faced a high cost of funds as interest rates soared following the OPEC oil embargo of 1973 (chapter 17). Deregulation by the Reagan administration allowed it to seek higher returns with riskier investments. S&Ls took advantage of more lenient accounting rules and expanded lending authority to engage in deals far outside their traditional expertise in home mortgage lending. Inept management and insider dealing at some S&Ls produced preposterous investments. Competition between many apartment complexes in the same area financed by the same S&L assured that none of them would be profitable. The cost of funds increased further as institutions competed with each other, and this required ever riskier investments.

This foolishness would not go unpunished indefinitely. From 1986 to 1989, the Federal Savings and Loan Insurance Corporation (FSLIC) would close or otherwise resolve 296 S&Ls with total assets of $125 billion. The number of federally insured S&Ls declined from 3,234 to 1,645 from 1986 to 1995.[3] A report by the United States League of Savings Institutions[4] would cite fifteen reasons for S&L failures, including seven for lack of regulation and supervision, and three for fraud or poor management. The Resolution Trust Corporation (RTC) was formed in 1989 to allow the federal government to bail out the thrift industry. According to Fraser, the RTC had $210 billion in assets by 1990,[5] more than those of any other corporation in America. The S&L bailout cost the taxpayers the equivalent of three years of private investment in plants and equipment. In addition to the S&L crisis, between 1980 and 1994 more than 1,600 banks insured by the FDIC were closed or received financial assistance.[6] The deregulation fox had guarded the financial hen house and left a pile of bones and feathers.

On Wall Street, the corporate takeover and buyout frenzy was ended by a federal investigation of illegal insider trading. Boesky, Milken, and others would go to prison. Predictably (chapter 14), government had to be called in to correct the problems of inadequate regulation. On October 17, 1987, the stock market crashed.[7] The Dow lost 23 percent, or 508 points, a record for a single day and twice the decline on "Black Tuesday" in 1929. Ironically, some attributed the crash to computer-generated sales designed to minimize risk.

In the broader economy, Reagan greatly benefited

from the collapse of oil prices in the mid-1980s (chapter 17). This reduced both energy costs and inflation, thus increasing consumer purchasing power. Unemployment had initially risen from 7.1 percent in 1980 under Jimmy Carter to over 10 percent between September 1982 and June 1983 under Reagan. But it would go down to 5.5 percent at the end of the Reagan era in 1988.[8] During that time, inflation would go from 12.5 percent to 4.4 percent.[9] Reagan's 1981 tax reductions, the largest in US history, had been followed by tax increases in 1982, also the largest in US history. But net tax reductions during the Reagan years yielded inadequate tax revenue to pay the government's bills. A 40 percent increase in peacetime defense spending,[10] the S&L government bailout, a surprisingly weak economy, and the net tax cuts produced a growing federal government deficit.

George H.W. Bush

Reagan was succeeded by his vice-president, George H.W. Bush,[11] who professed allegiance to Reagan's tax cut philosophy in the 1988 election, famously saying "read my lips, no new taxes." Bush was a genuine war hero in WWII after he became the youngest pilot in naval history in 1943. But he would be called on to show another type of courage as president.

Reagan and Bush were two very different kinds of Republicans. A Californian, Reagan advocated a Western style of "get the government off my back" conservatism associated with Arizona senator Barry Goldwater whom Reagan had campaigned for in the 1964 presidential election. Bush had moved to Texas after the war but represented a more moderate form of conservatism often associated with wealthy East-Coast Republicans like former vice president and New York governor Nelson Rockefeller. Bush and Rockefeller viewed government service more as a duty to serve the country than as a call to action against government.

Bush would have to clean up the damage caused by deregulation under Reagan. The Resolution Trust Corporation began operation in 1989, the first year of Bush's administration. Equally troublesome were budget deficits left over from the Reagan era. At $220 billion in 1990,[12] the deficit was triple that of 1980, Jimmy Carter's last year in office. Bush advocated a combination of spending cuts and tax increases but couldn't convince a Democratic Congress. Most Republicans favored spending cuts alone. Bush had a quandary that would affect his 1992 re-election chances. He had to choose between his Republican base, who remembered his "no new taxes" pledge, or raising taxes to reduce the budget deficit. He signed the Democrat's higher tax bill rather than precipitate an ideological battle with a veto. Despite his leadership in the 1991 Gulf War against Iraq (chapter 20), this tax increase and a mild recession in 1991 cost Bush the 1992 presidential election.

William Jefferson Clinton

William Jefferson Clinton (1946–) took office in 1993, the first baby boomer president.[13] While adhering to traditional Democratic progressive values, Clinton wanted to move his party more to the center. This came to be known as the "Third Way," a strategy later adopted by British Labor Party Prime Minister Tony Blair. Clinton's 1993 and 1994 budgets included both curbs in government spending and tax increases that reduced the federal deficit.

The election of a Republican Congress in 1994 set the stage for a grand ideological battle. This pitted Clinton, a Rhodes Scholar, against Republican Speaker of the House of Representatives Newt Gingrich, a history PhD. There was enough cooperation to produce the North American Free Trade Act (NAFTA), welfare reform, and an increased minimum wage. But ideological differences sharply divided the two parties, and any spending or taxation issue produced serious conflict. Congressional Republicans took the heat for a government shutdown for six days in November 1995 and another shutdown for twenty-one days from December 1995 to January 1996. This contributed to Clinton's re-election in 1996.

The possibility of damage from the ideological conflict in Clinton's second term was greatly reduced by the dot-com boom and the resulting spurt of economic activity. Throughout American history, the emergence of new technology such as railroads and automobiles has produced economic growth, jobs, and increased tax revenue. The late 1990s were no exception. The $70 billion budget surplus in 1998 was the first surplus since 1969.

Between 1981 and early 2001, the United States dodged a fiscal bullet as tensions rose between Republicans and Democrats over the levels of government spending and taxation. Reagan and Bush had agreed to raise taxes at times and Clinton had cut some spending.

But is there really a question of whether spending or taxation comes first? When the elected representatives of the American people vote to give the people something they want, then one of three things happens:

- Revenue is dedicated to pay for it. Payroll tax deductions for Social Security and Medicare are examples of dedicated revenue.
- It is paid for out of general revenues.
- The government incurs debt to pay for it.

"It" may be national defense, homeland security, road construction, or a social program. Unlike private sector budgets, where spending is a function of income over the long term, government income (i.e., taxation) is determined by government spending. When Pearl Harbor was bombed, no one said that the United States couldn't respond because our tax rates were already too high. The American people can get any government service they deem necessary. Their spending will determine the amount of tax revenue needed to pay the bills.

For decades, Americans did not pay taxes contemporaneously for government services but used debt financing. They assumed that economic growth would maintain the national debt at a fairly constant proportion of GNP. This may not be possible if there is inadequate growth or if politicians continue to buy votes by promising tax cuts. "Pay-as-you-go" taxation may be required in the future.

Chapter 22
George W. Bush

Republican George W. Bush took office as President on January 20, 2001,[1] after winning the hotly contested 2000 election from Bill Clinton's vice president, Al Gore. The US Supreme Court ruled in the case of *Bush vs. Gore* that the controversial Florida election results would stand, with Bush winning by 537 votes out of 6 million votes cast. This gave Bush a 271 to 266 vote victory in the Electoral College, even though Gore had received over 500,000 more votes than Bush in the popular election.

The Republican majorities in both houses of Congress that had fought Bill Clinton (chapter 21) were still in place after the 2000 election, so Bush was the wild card. Born in New Haven, Connecticut, Bush had moved to Texas as a child when his already wealthy parents went west to supplement their inherited fortunes with oil money.[*] A nickname-calling, back-slapping, easy-going sort, Bush was never known to take any particular interest in the great issues of the day, foreign or domestic. The most commonly heard refrain from close supporters in Texas in his campaigns for governor and president was that "his advisors will keep him straight."

Bush had worked on his father's losing 1992 re-election campaign, and he knew that tax increases were fatal to your political health in the Republican Party. In fact,

---

[*] A good source of information about George W. Bush's early life is Bill Minutaglio, *First Son* (New York: Three Rivers Press, 1999). However, the comments above are not from Minutaglio's book.

his conservative advisors told Bush that since government was "the problem," tax cuts were always in order. His administration reduced federal income tax rates in 2001. There was no widespread opposition to this, even though the tax cuts plus the end of the dot-com boom of the late 1990s would change a budget surplus from the Clinton administration to a budget deficit. The American people had heard so much anti-government rhetoric since the Reagan administration that they would salivate at the sound of the words "tax cut." Unlike Pavlov's dogs, however, Americans would be responsible for the budget deficits and increased national debt that resulted.

Tax Cuts and Spending Increases

The 9/11 terrorist attacks would dramatically increase the costs of national defense, homeland security, and intelligence-gathering, and would start the two longest wars in US history. The war in Afghanistan was intended to kill or capture al-Qaeda leaders, but the war in Iraq mainly increased terrorism and directed resources away from Afghanistan (chapter 20). The Bush administration reduced taxes again in 2003. The volunteer military had to risk death in these wars, but no living American would have to pay for them anytime soon. For the first time in American history, a major war (actually two wars) was fought without any sacrifices being asked of civilians.

It is virtually impossible to get a good estimate of the cost of the war on terrorism. Some defense funding comes from the base budget, while other money comes from supplemental appropriations. Intelligence's costs can come from the defense budget, homeland security, or supplemental funding. The *Washington Post* reported in 2011 that an extensive investigation by Dana Priest and William M. Arkin of domestic anti-terrorism efforts turned up a "top-secret world . . . so large, so unwieldy and so secretive that no one knows how much money it costs, how many people it employs, how many programs exist within it or exactly how many agencies do the same work."[2] Among other things, Priest and Arkin reported that about 854,000 people (about 1 in every 350 Americans) have top-secret security clearance and that analysts publish 50,000 intelligence reports a year. If these numbers are even close to being correct, then the resulting diseconomies of large scale may ensure that in this case, government may indeed be the problem and not the solution. Useful information can be lost in all the reports published and dollars spent.

In 2003, two expansions of Medicare were urged by the Bush administration and the Republican Congress. Medicare advantage plans injected private companies into the Medicare system (chapter 11), thus increasing costs. This Medicare modification was unfunded. A Medicare Part D drug plan was created and, of course, it too was unfunded. This program had the interesting provision that, unlike the Veterans' Administration or Wal-mart, Medicare would not be allowed to use its great buying power to get price reductions on drugs. The Medicare expansion combined lack of funding with built-in inefficiency, thus assuring financial problems in the future.

What is especially odd is that Republican ideologues have always opposed Medicare, typically referring to it as socialism. This huge Republican-supported expansion of Medicare in 2003 could be compared to a group of evangelical Christians funding a chain of abortion clinics. Of course, the critical fact was that everything in the Medicare bill was unfunded. This would allow Medicare opponents who voted for the Medicare expansion to tell Americans in the future that the program would have to be dramatically reduced because "we must live within our means."

Bush's declaration on May 1, 2003, that "major combat operations in Iraq have ended" would later be seen as a sign of incompetence. The infamous "Mission Accomplished" banner behind him on the deck of the aircraft carrier *Abraham Lincoln*[3] would serve as a symbol of Bush's detachment and lack of credibility as the war continued for many years. The war in Iraq was worse than pointless (chapter 20), but it was awkward for Americans to criticize it because of the nation's concerns for its military personnel who bravely did their duty. It didn't seem unreasonable to ask people safely on the home front to pay a few dollars to finance the wars.

Ideology and Katrina

In late August 2005, Hurricane Katrina had become a category 5 storm in the Gulf of Mexico. It would soon come ashore in Texas, Louisiana, Mississippi, Alabama, or Florida, and wherever it made landfall, it would be destructive. Lives and property would be destroyed, and emergency services compromised. Any of the five state governors might be called upon to provide disaster assis-

George W. Bush

tance, but the one chief executive who would definitely have to act was President George W. Bush.

On August 29, Katrina hit land in Mississippi just east of New Orleans. A tidal surge destroyed levees, flooding the city, but Bush was effectively a no-show for days. Bush seemed oblivious to any federal responsibility for disaster relief. When he casually flew over the disaster in Air Force One, Howard Fineman of *Newsweek* described the pictures of the "president as tourist, seemingly powerless as he peered down at the chaos." According to the *US News & World Report*, "White House political advisors admitted later 'It looked like he didn't know what was going on.'" **

When judging Bush's performance after Hurricane Katrina, it is important to remember that a basic tenet of conservative philosophy is that "government is not the solution, it is the problem" (Reagan, 1981). Conservatives want to minimize federal government responsibility, leaving more to the private sector, and to state and local governments. Aggressively aiding hurricane victims would be a dangerous first step up the slippery slope to human decency. The sight of New Orleans Democrats in neck-deep water waiting for federal government assistance thrilled the more rabid antigovernment ideologues, until they realized that Katrina was a public relations disaster for Bush.

After Katrina, Americans would reassess Bush and his administration's policies. The repeated tax cuts in

---

** These quotes are from Fineman, "A Storm-Tossed Boss," *Newsweek*, September 19, 2005, and "Anatomy of a Disaster," *U.S. News & World Report*, September 26, 2005.

the face of dramatically increased demand for government services would compromise federal government finances long after Bush left office. When combined with the cynical, unfunded expansions of Medicare, Bush's fiscal policies looked like an assault on the US government. Republicans had abandoned Ronald Reagan's principles. No matter how much Reagan wanted to shrink government and reduce taxes, he had not allowed ideology to destroy the country. Reagan agreed to tax increases when necessary.

The public began to recognize the moral vacuum in anti-government, pro-market ideology. It was no coincidence that the philosopher Ayn Rand was an atheist. She was the leading proponent of Objectivism, the notion that self-interest should guide both personal and economic decisions. To accept responsibility for helping your fellow man, it was not necessary to be a believer. You simply had to know that people are more important than money. And the Fallacy of Composition (chapter 5) reminds us that acting solely in one's own self interest can have unintended consequences.

The Katrina disaster affected Americans emotionally, and they responded in many ways, giving their time, money, and other resources. They had also responded to the 9/11 terrorist attacks. Many even enlisted in the military. But Americans don't know how to respond to an economic assault. Budget deficits, tax cuts, national debt, unemployment, investment, growth, and stimulus plans seem to be complicated concepts.

Perhaps common sense is the best guide in the long run for solving economic problems. If you don't pay for it, you don't get it. If money is concentrated in just a few places, then it's not going to circulate very much in the broader economy. If an economy goes into a deep hole, then there is little incentive for economic investment. It is always better to anticipate and prevent problems, than to clean up the mess after they happen. In a democracy, injustice is corrected at the ballot box, not in the streets.

The wars would linger far beyond Bush's second term in office. Memories of the Katrina fiasco would not soon go away, either. But the Bush administration still had one thing going for it: the housing market. Low mortgage interest rates and minimal regulation in the financial sector were producing a boom in home sales and construction. Other than war-time spending, nothing revs up an economy like commercial and residential real estate activity. Construction workers, real estate agents, home appraisers, movers, furniture and appliance salesmen, landscapers, attorneys, bankers, investment bankers, home inspectors, insurance agents, credit-rating agencies, and many other people and companies were all busy growing America. This was precisely how tax cuts, deregulation, and the invisible hand of markets were supposed to work.

Chapter 23
The Great Recession

The Federal Reserve System lowered interest rates after the end of the dot-com boom and following the 9/11 terrorist attacks in order to spur economic activity. Financing of big-ticket items like televisions, appliances, and cars became much cheaper. What was surprising was that lower interest rates seemed to create a huge real estate boom. Residential and commercial real estate purchases are financed with long-term borrowing, and long-term loans are inherently risky (chapter 7). The due diligence required of mortgage lenders to justify these loans was largely unaffected by lower interest rates. Yet by 2002, money was readily available for home purchases all across the country.

Anyone could get a mortgage as easily as they could get a credit card. TV ads said "come in and get approved for a home loan in thirty minutes." Apparently, someone had written a computer program that streamlined the arduous application process. Income documents, credit checks, asset verification, and due diligence were things of the past. Mortgage loan officers had become like used car salesmen. "What do I have to do to put you in this little $300,000 bungalow?" They were flexible. Subprime, adjustable-rate, no-down-payment, and interest-only loans were available.

Banks and other lenders are merely originators of mortgage loans. They don't keep the loans but sell them into securitized mortgage pools called collateralized debt obligations (CDOs). These can be sold all over the world to financial institutions which can then use the CDOs as collateral for further borrowing. Thus a home mortgage in Arizona might be part of a CDO used by a bank in Europe to borrow money, which, in turn, could be used to make further home loans. With no effective government regulations and loose lending standards, by 2002, financial institutions everywhere were interconnected by this process of mortgage securitization.

Investment banks were the driving force in the CDO creation process and encouraged commercial banks and other mortgage lenders to make home loans, the raw material of CDOs. This process was so lucrative that investment banks got directly into making mortgages. For example, in December 2006, Merrill Lynch paid $1.3 billion for First Franklin,[1] one of the country's largest subprime mortgage companies. Also, many financial institutions sold credit default swaps (CDSs). These were derivatives (chapter 9) used to insure CDOs and other financial instruments held by banks around the world. Since derivatives were unregulated financial products, there was no guarantee that they were backed by any reserves.

The whole worldwide system of CDOs and CDSs rested on the shaky foundation of loose mortgage lending standards, particularly in the United States. Subprime loans were often improperly mixed with prime loans in CDOs. But unregulated credit rating agencies like Moody's and Standards & Poor's made no distinction between CDOs, giving all of them high investment grade ratings.

These problems were compounded by excessive home prices in some parts of the United States. Easy mortgage money had spurred home sales, raising prices despite new construction. Home buyers could get too much house at too high a price with no down payment and an adjustable-rate mortgage. They received assurances that increasing real estate prices and tax advantages from interest and property tax deductions would more than make up for any future increase in monthly payments. Ever-increasing housing prices were required to keep this scheme going. But housing prices couldn't go up forever.

The Real Estate Bubble Bursts

In February 2007, CNN Money reported that a "jump in defaults of high-risk borrowers" was becoming impossible to ignore.[2] During 2007, lenders began foreclosures on 1.3 million properties, with another 2.3 million foreclosures in 2008.[3] But home mortgages were the assets underlying the value of mortgage securities. As the number of foreclosures mounted from 2007 to 2008, the loss of asset value created a crisis in the financial sector. Financial firms were highly leveraged institutions (chapter 6), particularly investment banks which might borrow thirty times as much as they contributed in equity. Moreover, the assets of one financial firm were often the liabilities of another. The interconnected web of financial transactions on Wall Street meant that the failure of one large company could precipitate a domino-like collapse of the whole financial system.

Fear swept Wall Street. Goldman Sachs, the street's

most prominent investment banking firm, spent $150 million to buy derivatives to insure itself against default on $2.5 billion in debt from AIG, the world's largest insurance company.[4] AIG was a leading seller of CDSs, the unregulated derivatives that supposedly insured CDOs. Short-sellers began preying on investment banks by borrowing their stock and selling it in order to drive the stock price down. Short-sellers would profit by buying the stock back at lower prices.

No business resisted government regulation more than financial firms. They often profited from the public's ignorance of complex financial instruments like adjustable-rate mortgages and derivatives. But in 2008, investment bankers were begging for government regulators to stop short-sellers from driving their stock prices down. According to Andrew Ross Sorkin, author of *Too Big to Fail*, one prominent Wall Street manager pleaded with George Bush's Treasury Secretary, Hank Paulsen, "People are shorting financial institutions, they're withdrawing money from brokerage firms . . . Everybody is just pursuing his self-interest. You have to do something."[5]

In March, 2008, the Federal Reserve System had engineered J.P. Morgan's purchase of Bear Stearns, a large investment bank with considerable derivative exposure. The Fed had guaranteed $29 billion in Bear Stearns debt to make the deal go through.[6] But Secretary Paulsen, the former chairman of Goldman Sachs, Fed Chairman Ben Bernanke, New York Fed President Tim Geithner, and others in government worried that other financial firms might expect to be bailed out. They were concerned with "moral hazard," the notion that private firms could keep the rewards of successful risky investments but could be expected to be bailed out from the government when risky investments failed. So when Lehmann Brothers, another large investment bank, found itself in trouble, it was allowed to fail. Lehmann's bankruptcy on September 15, 2008, was the largest in US history and sent shock waves through the financial world, magnifying the crisis.

Something had to be done. Some financial firms were just too big to fail. AIG, for example, had sold 12,000 individual derivative contracts worth $2.7 trillion.[7] There were hundreds of trillions of dollars' worth of derivatives in the world, each of which was backed by financial firms whose assets were often insured only by derivatives themselves. So in September, 2008, the Bush administration recommended the Troubled Asset Relief Program (TARP) to Congress. When finally approved, it would be a $700 billion government bailout of the financial system put together by an administration dominated largely by pro-free market, anti-government ideologues.

Democratic Congressmen Barney Frank noted that between saving Bear Stearns and the TARP bailout, the restraint of "moral hazard" had lasted precisely one day: September 15, the day Lehmann Brothers filed for bankruptcy. Frank quipped that September 15 should be called "Free Market Day." He said that "the national commitment to the free market lasted one day. It was Monday."[8]

The Disaster Spreads

Many financial firms would go bankrupt or be absorbed by other companies. Washington Mutual and

Countrywide Savings disappeared. Merrill Lynch would be bought by Bank of America. Among non-financial companies, Circuit City, Linens 'n Things, and Mervyn's were closed; Chrysler and General Motors borrowed TARP money from the Bush administration. People would lose their jobs as business activity slowed, partly due to lack of available credit in the financial sector.

There were actually three types of mortgage defaults in the Great Recession:

- Loans with either adjustable-rate or interest-only mortgages, which people could not afford after the loans adjusted to conventional loans with market or above-market rates. The above-market rates compensated lenders for the below-market "teaser" rates before the adjustment. This type of loan default signaled the start of the Great Recession.
- Loans on which people chose to default because they found themselves "under-water," owing more than their house was worth. This often occurred in neighborhoods in which many people couldn't continue paying adjustable-rate loans and put their homes on the market at distressed prices. This lowered all nearby home prices.
- Loans to people who had lost their jobs and couldn't continue paying on their mortgage even though they may have borrowed prudently.

Mortgage defaults due to "under-water" loans or unemployment would continue for years. The housing bubble in the middle of Bush's two terms in office only temporarily increased home ownership. According to the 2010 census, home ownership actually decreased by

1.1 percent from 2000 to 2010, the largest drop-off since the Great Depression.[9] In the stock market, the Dow went from a high exceeding 14,000 in October 2007 to a low of about 6,600 in March 2009.[10] Unemployment would hit 10.1 percent by October 2009, the highest since the Reagan administration.[11]

Note that unemployment peaked after the official recession, which lasted from December 2007 to June 2009. Chapter 15 explained that economic misery such as high unemployment can continue after the end of the period of declining output that economists use to define a recession. In a steep economic downturn like the Great Recession, business people will act in their own self-interests to cut costs. They lay people off, which increases unemployment and reduces consumption. This inadvertent application of the Fallacy of Composition (chapter 5) just makes things worse. There is no automatic, internal mechanism in a market economy to correct a steep downturn.

Reduced economic activity in the Great Recession, the expense of the wars in Afghanistan and Iraq, and previous tax cuts, would create a deficit of more than $500 billion for Bush's successor in 2009. This would be the highest budget deficit in history, although several deficits were higher as a percentage of the overall economy in the Reagan and George H. W. Bush administrations. The American people would feel the impact of the Great Recession for many years to come.

With the fiasco in Iraq and his neglect during Hurricane Katrina, Bush's performance in office had left historians unimpressed. In 2006, 744 professional historians surveyed by Sienna College rated Bush as follows: "below average" 24 percent, "failure" 58 percent.[12] As it became obvious in 2008 that the Great Recession would be by far the worst economic downturn since the Great Depression, a *USA Today* poll gave Bush an approval rating of only 28 percent with 69 percent expressing disapproval.[13]

Chapter 24
The Causes of the Great Recession

It became clear in 2006 that the real estate bubble could not be maintained by ever-increasing home prices. The next year, massive numbers of foreclosures crippled the economy so much that by December 2007, the United States was formally in a recession. The devastation to the financial sector caused by the diminished value of mortgage-backed securities was alleviated by the TARP program in 2008, but the economy would be hurt badly for many years to come. This was a source of humiliation to a Congress and to a presidential administration that espoused the virtues of free markets unfettered by government. Every religion has a branch of its theology called apologetics, which serves to explain away doctrinal problems. Free-market ideology is no exception. The search for scapegoats began.

Some alleged causes of the economic crisis can be easily dismissed. Securitized mortgages had been around for generations, and—properly done (!)—they, give mortgage lenders increased liquidity, geographic diversity, and lower interest rates (chapter 7). Subprime loans had been available for years and offered lenders higher returns to compensate for higher risks. More importantly, at $2 trillion, subprime lending was just a small part of the $14 trillion US mortgage market.[1] The Community Reinvestment Act (CRA), a "Jimmy Carter era law" designed to encourage home ownership, was a favorite target. Blaming Jimmy Carter for the economic problems of the 1970s (chapter 18) that had started four years before Carter took office had worked well for Ronald Reagan, so why not try it again? But a 2009 analysis by the Federal Reserve Bank of Dallas determined that the CRA was not to blame for the mortgage loan crisis.[2] The CRA rules had been in effect years before the mortgage crisis and had not caused the problems. Since 2009, there have been numerous lawsuits against the financial sector filed by the federal government and all of the state-attorneys-general. But none of the banks or the thousands of people involved in mortgage lending or securitization has invoked the CRA as the "devil made me do it" defense.

Borrowers: Victims or Perpetrators?

It has been suggested that many borrowers were taking advantage of loose lending standards to do cash-out refinancing or to make speculative purchases with the intention of flipping, or reselling, their homes but this was far from the norm. The overwhelming majority of borrowers were just ordinary Americans who knew nothing about mortgage financing. They should have been able to rely on lenders for honest information. If people are sick, they don't have to first go to medical school before seeing a doctor. If they want to finance a home, they shouldn't have to go to business school and study finance before seeking a loan. People know little about medicine. They know even less about finance. It is an unfortunate fact that hundreds of thousands of ordinary people should have been told, before they signed their adjustable-rate loan documents, that they would be

THE CAUSES OF THE GREAT RECESSION

in grave danger of default when their monthly payments increased in a year or two.

Yet claims of chicanery persisted. The "scam" that borrowers allegedly pulled off went something like this: An ordinary American couple found a home they liked, and a real estate agent told them that they shouldn't pay rent but should have the advantages of home ownership. They paid a loan origination fee and other closing costs while getting a no-down-payment, adjustable-rate mortgage. They paid to move into their newly financed home. They paid to have utilities connected. They paid for window treatments, extra furniture, and decorative items. They paid to improve the yard and for outdoor furniture. They paid their monthly mortgage payments for about two years. But when the interest rate adjusted upward, they could not afford the payments any longer. They paid to move out. This was some scam!

Since long-term lending is inherently risky (chapter 7), mortgage lending was historically the most conservative area of commercial banking. So what happened in the financial sector that produced the mortgage crisis? Credit card lending provides a clue. By the early 2000s, credit card issuers had been running amok for years, gouging card-holders with high interest rates, fees, and penalties. Mounting credit card debt had entrapped many consumers in a vicious cycle of debt repayment, alternating with calamities like medical problems, unemployment, and home and auto repairs. But borrowers had one ultimate remedy to their debt problems: bankruptcy protection.

Filing for bankruptcy allowed people to shed long-term financial burdens that could destroy a life. Bankruptcy protection is a hallmark of a civilized society, an end to the onerous debts and poorhouses that the English novelist Charles Dickens had written about. And bankruptcy laws were also an essential feature of a fair and functional free-market economy. The existence of such laws constrained financial institutions to prudent lending practices. This protected borrowers, lenders, and the entire country. But in the George W. Bush administration and the Republican Congress, credit card issuers found sympathy for the notion that borrowers alone should be held accountable for bad debts, even though low lending standards had allowed everyone and his dog to get one or more credit cards. The prolonged whining of the financial sector culminated in the Bankruptcy Abuse Prevention and Consumer Protection Act of 2005. This Act had nothing directly to do with the mortgage lending crisis, but it reinforced the mentality in the financial sector that borrowers were fair game and that lenders were not to blame. It was OK to apply the loose standards of credit card lending to mortgage loans. But there was a huge difference between burdening a consumer with thousands of dollars of credit card debt and burdening the consumer with hundreds of thousands of dollars of mortgage debt they could never repay.

Many financial regulations were eliminated in the 1980s by Ronald Reagan and further loosened in the 1990s. But in the George W. Bush administration, Wall Street knew that the White House and both houses of Congress were controlled by ideologues who would let the free market work unfettered by government. So lack of restraint in the financial sector became the norm. Investment banks encouraged mortgage lending in order to create and sell securitized mortgages. Mortgage lenders cheerfully loaned money to anybody who could breathe knowing that they could dump their lending mistakes into mortgage securities. Credit rating agencies gleefully profited by giving every piece of paper a high investment grade rating. Not willing to lose business, home appraisers complied with the trend of ever-increasing housing prices. The bubble expanded until it burst.

Fannie Mae

The history of a government-sponsored enterprise (GSE) provides the ultimate insight into the underlying causes of the Great Recession. The Federal National Mortgage Association (FNMA), commonly called Fannie Mae, was created in 1938 to encourage home ownership by forming a secondary market for home loans. This allowed loans to be repackaged into mortgage-backed securities (MBSs). By 1968, Fannie Mae was a publicly traded company with common stock owned by private investors.[3] Since it retained an "implicit" guarantee of federal government support, Fannie Mae was able to borrow money more cheaply than other private sector companies. In this regard, Fannie Mae was no different than any other private sector firm which availed itself of any government benefit it could. State, county, and local governments across the nation offered tax abatements, infrastructure improvements, and even money for construction projects to businesses to encourage them to stay or to build in an area. Government bonds were even used to back athletic facilities which greatly enhanced the value and profitability of professional sports franchises. Businesses are always against government—except when they can benefit from government.

Even after becoming a private company, Fannie Mae was able to maintain its high underwriting standards. It accepted only well-documented, prudent loans from mortgage originators like commercial banks. But by the early part of the twenty-first century, Fannie Mae had to compete with other mortgage securitizers. These investment bank securitizers were willing to accept lower lending standards because, unlike Fannie Mae, they retained minimal risk. They either sold off the mortgage-backed securities or bought derivatives that purported to insure the MBSs. Under pressure from its shareholders and high-level managers making investment banker-style compensation, Fannie Mae tried to maintain market share by lowering its standards. It then found itself inundated with nebulous mortgage-backed securities made up of poorly documented and ill-conceived loans. (In September, 2011, the US government would sue seventeen financial institutions that had sold Fannie Mae and the smaller GSE, Freddie Mac, nearly $200 billion in mortgage-backed securities that later soured.)[4]

When the home mortgage crisis hit, Fannie Mae was burdened by non-performing loans, its stock price collapsed, and on September 7, 2008, it was placed into conservatorship by the Federal Housing Finance Agency.[5] While Fannie Mae was saved in a different manner than AIG and other financial firms, it too was bailed out by

The Causes of the Great Recession

the government. Fannie Mae provides a test of sorts that defines the true causes of the Great Recession. To the extent that Fannie Mae operated as a government agency, securitizing mortgages and encouraging home ownership, it functioned properly. Only when its shareholders and highly paid managers succumbed to unrestrained greed did it acquiesce to low lending standards.

The public expects higher standards from government employees than it does from private sector workers motivated only by money (chapter 14). High-ranking managers at Fannie Mae did not make federal civil service salaries, or even cabinet-level or presidential salaries. They made investment bankers' incomes. There have been insinuations that Fannie Mae as a government agency caused the Great Recession, but the truth is precisely the opposite. It was Fannie Mae's status as a private firm, with self-serving managers and shareholders seeking private sector rewards that caused it to become part of the problem.

Fannie Mae and Freddie Mac executives responsible for these failures left without severance pay, but other private sector executives brought in to clean up the mess were given huge compensation packages.[6] Of course, this created further controversy, since it was reminiscent of the large retention bonuses often paid to executives of bankrupt companies to avoid high levels of turnover except now, the public was paying. Perhaps the lesson for taxpayers is that Wall Street labor is expensive, whether it is hired to straighten out a disaster or to create one.

Greed and inadequate government regulation caused the Great Recession. While any lack of necessary regulation invites exploitation, an announcement by a presidential administration that regulation is bad is an invitation to businesses to take advantage of any loose regulatory constraints. Examples include the savings and loan debacle and the insider trading and stock manipulation on Wall Street (chapter 21) during the Reagan administration. After Reagan, President George H. W. Bush was too busy cleaning up the financial mess to start another disaster with antiregulatory rhetoric. During the Clinton administration, Treasury Secretary Robert Rubin, a former Goldman Sachs manager, and Fed Chairman Alan Greenspan were strong free market advocates and influenced Clinton's "Third Way" policies.

In 1998, a small hedge fund in Greenwich, Connecticut, called Long-Term Capital Management (LTCM) collapsed, threatening to wreak havoc in world financial markets when it could not meet debt repayment obligations as its investments failed.[*] LTCM's managers included some of the top Wall Street traders and best financial experts in the world. It used derivatives, option trading, and ultra-high leverage to make enormous profits for a few years. But when its economic models ultimately failed, a consortium of financial institutions had to pool their resources to save the financial markets. Yet the fact that just one little company could create a potentially earth-shattering financial disaster did not convince free market advocates like Rubin and Greenspan to accept any regulation of derivatives.

The Great Recession was the predictable result of

---

[*] LTCM is discussed in Roger Lowenstein, *When Genius Failed* (New York: Random House, 2000).

the lack of restraint on the normal impulses of greed and self-interest that motivate market activity. Accumulated empirical evidence strongly suggests that with sufficiently inadequate regulation, Americans can count on recurring large-scale problems in the financial sector, particularly if government leaders publicly oppose any "government interference" in the market. If you want to bet on the next financial crisis, put your money on the $700 trillion, largely unregulated world derivative market. Ironically, massive losses by ordinary people in recent years on their homes and investments may reduce criminal behavior in the financial sector for a while.

Certainly, there is a big lesson that can be learned from the mortgage crisis. For the same reason commercial banks do not advertise weaknesses in their security systems, government leaders should not invite exploitation of ordinary citizens by speaking openly of any general ideological aversion to financial regulation.

Chapter 25
Barack Obama

Suppose there were a chief executive officer's job opening at a large national corporation that provided essential services to vast numbers of people. Everyone in the United States used some of the company's services and almost every service it provided was needed by large numbers of Americans. But about half of its shareholders and half of the members of its board of directors wanted to reduce the company's size, claiming that it was too big and inefficient. They encouraged customers not to pay their bills. For about thirty years, they had tried to reduce the amount that customers were charged. This, combined with ever-increasing demand for the company's services, had created a rising and ultimately unsustainable corporate debt.

The new CEO would have to deal with two squabbling factions: one opposing income, the other demanding services. To make matters worse, nearly half of the company's customers were members of both factions at the same time. Additionally, the company had just experienced an eight-year period of dramatically increased demand by all of its customers, including those who insisted on reducing its revenue. The CEO's job paid far less than that of chief executives at other large companies. It offered neither bonuses nor stock options, but—not surprisingly—it offered considerable personal security protection.

Such was the state of the US Government at the time

of the 2008 presidential election. If the presidency was a high-level corporate job, nobody would want it. But political parties exist to get their members elected to as many public offices as possible. And unlike members of Congress, the president controls vast patronage. The Washington, DC, area has numerous upscale rental houses and lots of nice homes that change ownership with each election. Anyone who gets elected president will get their name in the history books.

The big issues in the 2008 election were the policies of President George W. Bush and his administration (chapter 22). Many Americans were disillusioned by the superfluous war in Iraq (chapter 20), Bush's perceived negligence after Hurricane Katrina, the collapse of the economy (chapter 23) following years of unrestrained mortgage lending (chapter 24), and increasing unemployment and budget deficits. There was precious little for the winner of the election to look forward to. And since Americans seemed prone to short-term thinking, the new president would eventually be blamed for all the mistakes of the past.

When the Republican candidate, Senator John McCain of Arizona, could not convince the voters that his policies were any different than Bush's, the American people elected Senator Barack Obama (1961–) to the White House.[1] The tall, lanky Democratic senator from Illinois, with his calm demeanor and oratorical gifts, invited comparisons to Abraham Lincoln. With the financial collapse that started in 2007 likely to produce economic devastation for many years to come, a growing national debt, and ever-intensifying partisan bickering, the United

States faced perhaps its greatest domestic conflict since the Civil War.

The nation had experienced increasing ideological differences since the 1980 presidential election. Jimmy Carter had lost partly because he could not convince Americans to roll up their sleeves and work to conserve energy in order to resist the economic problems caused by the OPEC oil embargo. Ronald Reagan had won because he was perhaps a little too convincing in his claims that mere external forces should not diminish Americans' standard of living. And according to Reagan, the real enemy was the US government. Reagan's simple catch phrase, "Government is not the solution, it is the problem," had become the guiding philosophy of many conservatives. This phrase could be wielded to justify "starving the beast" of revenue by cutting taxes. It was simplistic enough to justify ending or reducing any social program including Medicare and Social Security. It would be used to resist children's health care, food stamps, disaster relief, and anything that Americans did to help themselves through government.

For Democrats, no such simple phrase was possible. Each government action had to be justified separately. Some things were good (food stamps for poor people), while others were bad (tax breaks for rich hedge fund managers). But 2009, President Obama's first year in office, presented a unique opportunity for Democrats. The sweeping failures of the Bush administration were on a political and economic silver platter ready to be served up to Americans as proof that anti-government policy was against the best interests of most people. It would be easy now to reset the terms of public discourse from the simplistic "all government is bad" to the much more reasonable "some government programs and actions are essential to the American people."

Everyone—Democrats, Independents, even Republicans—expected the eloquent Obama to use this opportunity to define his principled and pragmatic opposition to the policies of the past. And he proceeded to say—nothing! No reminders of the massive failures of the Bush administration. No calls for a change in the nation's view of government. Nothing! But why? Perhaps it was Obama's ingrained tendency to seek cooperation and reconciliation. But it soon became apparent that the sole objective of Republicans was to make Obama a one-term president. They were certainly not going to reward him for his attempts at bipartisan compromise. In addition, it appeared that it took time for Obama and his family to adjust to life in the White House. A move is difficult for any family with young children. But making use of this rare opportunity to refute the opposition's anti-government philosophy was not optional. For years, the notion that government was bad had been a reference point for many Americans. By not refuting this, Obama had guaranteed that any domestic program he advocated, no matter how necessary, would be ridiculed as just another example of excessive government.

The Obama Stimulus

The first domestic priority for the new president was the Great Recession he inherited from the Bush administration. This collapse in the economy was too steep to be called a "normal" downturn in the business cycle (chapter 15). It had domestic causes: the greed and lack of regulation that precipitated the mortgage crisis. But it could not be corrected by Federal Reserve System actions alone. The only other such steep downturn in modern American history, the Great Depression, required correction by government fiscal policy in the form of a stimulus policy that ultimately included World War II spending.

A stimulus is designed to inject federal money into the economy, but it is a more focused spending plan than ordinary government deficit spending. In the short term, any stimulus plan can save, and even create, jobs. But the goal is to jump-start the economy and spur long-term growth. Two things are required: (1) the stimulus plan must be large enough to move a huge economy (World War II was a bit of overkill) and (2) the stimulus must be widely accepted. This second feature is essential since, ultimately, individual consumers must be encouraged to spend, businesses must become confident enough to hire and expand, and investors must be optimistic enough of future growth to shift money from financial investments to economic investments.

Obama's stimulus plan, the American Recovery and Reinvestment Act of 2009, was an $800 billion collection of programs ranging from payroll tax cuts, extended benefits and health insurance for the unemployed, to higher education grants, and payments to cities to prevent layoffs of teachers and policemen. While it certainly kept unemployment down, it was not large enough to jump-start the huge US economy. And persistent, and predictable, Republican criticism precluded any positive psychological boost that would encourage people to either spend or invest in new economic activity. This was not the early 1940s, when widespread patriotism in support of the war also inadvertently supported an economic stimulus. This was 2009, when political gains were deemed more important than any bipartisan attempt to restore the economy.

Health Care Reform

Health care was another big issue in the United States. Millions of Americans lacked the medical insurance needed to get routine care, and people clogged hospital emergency rooms trying to get help. Compared to other advanced industrialized nations, the American health care system was expensive and inefficient. In 2006–07, the United States had 96 preventable deaths per 100,000 people compared to 55 per 100,000 in France.[2] Other countries like Ireland and Great Britain which previously had higher mortality rates than the United States, now had lower rates.

Health care costs had been rising faster than the rate of inflation in the United States for years. This was partly due to advances in medicine that offered patients new, and often expensive, forms of treatment. Additionally, because easing pain and suffering and preventing death are so important, people tend not to resist rising medical costs like they would steeply increasing costs in optional goods and services, such as golf clubs and spa treatments. Economists say that demand for necessities like health care for which there is no substitute is "inelastic." Demand for more frivolous things, or for goods which have a substitute (beef, chicken, pork, or fish), is said to be "elastic."

High health care costs and large numbers of uninsured Americans had produced a crisis that affected many people. It also adversely affected any business not in the health care field. If people were spending a higher proportion of their money on medical care each year, then the well-known "income effect" (chapter 17) dictated that they would have less money to spend on other things. Pizza parlors, furniture stores, manicurists, amusement parks, car washes, and golf courses would have less business if nothing was done to rein in health care costs.

Many Democrats preferred a single-payer insurance plan, both allowing those who "could not" get insurance and requiring those who "would not" get insurance, to use the established Medicare system. Forcing the voluntarily uninsured to get insurance—a Republican idea— would protect other Americans from the inevitable costs these people would impose on taxpayers. But Republicans opposed the single-payer plan as simply more big government. President Obama sought compromise by patterning a health care reform bill after that of former Republican Governor Mitt Romney in Massachusetts. Obama's plan, the Patient Protection and Affordable Care Act, became law in 2010. Once again, Obama's lapse in 2009 of not making a case for government involvement in solving problems came back to haunt him. Since the government was the enemy, Republicans would not cooperate in formulating a health care plan and they ridiculed the President's plan as just another large federal program. Despite its origins, Republicans derided the plan as "Obamacare."

Meanwhile, there were almost daily reminders in the news that the ongoing economic crisis had been caused by both sloppy mortgage lending practices and devious activities in the financial sector from 2002 to 2006. The Securities and Exchange Commission (SEC) reached settlements with some of the nation's largest financial institutions over their practice of assembling mortgage-backed securities composed of poor quality loans, selling them as good investments, and then placing bets in the market against them.[3] In 2010–11, JPMorgan Chase ($153.6 million), Citigroup ($285 million), and Goldman Sachs ($550 million) agreed to settlements. By October, 2011, the SEC had begun investigating ten credit rating agencies over their credit rating practices.[4] Many MBSs with high investment grade ratings had lost considerable value in 2007–08.

The housing markets were still in turmoil, with millions of homeowners either in foreclosure or behind in their mortgage payments. Not surprisingly, the same financial institutions that had engaged in slovenly lending practices during the 2002–06 real estate bubble (chapter 24) had not bothered to properly process routine paperwork documenting the disposition of mortgages as they were sold into MBSs. As a result, banks had difficulty completing foreclosures. Houses could not be resold, and borrowers as well as banks were in limbo. Some unemployed Americans couldn't accept job offers elsewhere in the country because they couldn't get out from under existing mortgages.

The mortgage crisis had become a nationwide debt crisis that could not be resolved due to sloppy, and sometimes illegally processed, loan documents. By 2011, all fifty state attorneys-general were trying to reach settlements with banks across the country to either get homeowners relief or to resolve foreclosures.[5] A settlement with just five of the major banks—Bank of America, JPMorgan Chase, Wells Fargo, Citigroup, and Ally Financial—could reach as high as $20 billion. All of this chaos in the financial sector was a reminder that the Bush administration's TARP program had "worked" by improving the balance sheets of banks in order to keep the banks from going under. However, TARP did not address the underlying problems: the bad loans and devalued mortgage securities that had come to be called "toxic assets." These would not just go away.

The Consumer Financial Protection Bureau

The collapse of the national economy due to lack of government regulations during the 2002–06 real estate bubble as well as previous problems with inadequate regulation would seem to suggest some obvious remedies. But throughout history, common sense and logic have often fallen victim to religious superstition. Idols must be worshipped, virgins must be sacrificed, and anti-government zealots must oppose all regulation. The powerful and well-funded financial sector lobbyists resisted any regulatory attempts by the Obama administration. In particular, they strongly opposed the Consumer Financial Protection Bureau (CFPB), which was created to restrict abusive and unfair financial practices, promote financial education, and receive complaints from consumers.

Other than the CFPB, the Obama administration's lack of success in achieving financial regulatory reform reflected the difficulty of getting the financial sector and its congressional supporters to cooperate. However, the administration came down hard on the oil industry after the 2010 explosion at the BP deep water Macondo well. Drilling operations were shut down across the Gulf of Mexico, even at shallow and moderate water depth locations where the industry had a good track record. This was particularly unfortunate because oil and gas exploration was one of the few bright spots generating jobs and investment in an otherwise sluggish economy.

Foreign Policy

Any assessment of Barack Obama's domestic policies must take into consideration the impact of the strong Republican opposition's commitment to keep government from working. Obama's stimulus plan kept the country from sinking into a depression, but it and every other domestic action the president took were relentlessly attacked as just more big government. However, Obama had noteworthy success in the conduct of foreign wars, an area where there was considerably less partisan opposition. Under his aggressive leadership, the military successfully attacked and killed several top al-Qaeda leaders, including Osama bin Laden. While in the Senate, Obama had opposed the Iraq War (chapter 20). This war was the greatest foreign policy mistake in American history. Under Obama, troops were out of Iraq by December 2011. The United States was negotiating to maintain a ground combat presence in nearby Kuwait, as well as naval warships in the Persian Gulf.[6] Whether troops were withdrawn from Iraq in 2011, 2021, or 2031, the country would be threatened by terrorists, and in danger of a civil war between Shiite and Sunni Muslims. But Iraq is now an Iraqi problem.

Obama's use of limited American manpower to help overthrow long-time dictator Muammar Gaddafi's regime in Libya is an example of the diplomacy and limited resource (DLR) strategy described in chapter 20. The United States and its allies were able to accomplish this without the risk of massive casualties or the expenditure of huge sums of money as in Vietnam and Iraq (2003). The complexities of US involvement in Libya and in Middle East uprisings in Egypt and Syria should serve as a warning to Americans that simplistic military intervention was largely a thing of the past.

Americans are aware of the dangers of war policies and economic policies motivated by ideology. But extremists in the US House of Representatives, from gerrymandered, one-party congressional districts, threats of filibusters in the Senate, and ID laws designed to prevent qualified people from voting have jeopardized the nation's status as a functional democracy. This only benefits anti-American-government ideologues. Barack Obama's reelection in 2012 could be seen as a rejection of this hyper-partisan view. Most Americans were ready to put political bickering behind them and to direct attention and resources to solving the country's problems.

Unfortunately, Republican obstructionism continued after the 2012 election. The GOP had refused to participate in health care reform in 2010 even though, historically, members of both parties agreed that something needed to be done. Instead, Republicans chose to use the issue for political gain. The GOP claimed that the law was unworkable but offered no alternative plan for the needs of the uninsured. In August 2013, Republicans shut down the federal government in protest. Politically, the nation had made no progress since the Republicans had shut down government twice in the Clinton administration.

Part V
America's Problems in Context

A common pastime familiar to all Americans is the great tradition of getting together with family or friends and saying stupid things while congratulating each other on how smart we are. For example: "Things should be like they were in the 1950s and 1960s." Yes, why can't all our global competitors simply disappear? Or perhaps: "I always knew that we could get more government services while paying fewer taxes." So maybe, one day, retail stores will also sell us everything below cost. Then there is: "We should shrink government down to nothing." I'm sure we will all feel a lot safer without a defense department or a police force.

Examples abound. One of my favorites is: "We should keep Medicare the same for voters fifty-five years old or older, but we should phase it out for younger people." I always suspected that people fifty-four and younger were physiologically different from their elders. These people will never get old and they will never get sick. And of course, the perennial favorite: "We don't need government. We should let the free market handle everything." All of us know that economic activity motivated by private sector supply and demand (e.g., dealing drugs and prostitution) is good. But government activity (e.g., military service, teaching school, or being an astronaut) is bad. The American people need to get a grip on the political and economic reality around them and make the hard choices necessary to correct the nation's problems and to ensure future economic prosperity.

Chapter 26
The Global Economy

The first OPEC oil embargo in 1973 signaled the end of the Age of Delusion (chapter 16). It was an economic shot-across-the-bow warning the United States that it was no longer a self-contained economy. OPEC interfered with oil markets partly because of disdain by many of its Arab countries for America's policy supporting Israel. But that was less important than the fact that third-world oil producers could have such a devastating effect on the US economy (chapter 17). Of more long-term significance was the rise of Japan to become the world's second largest economy. This was the beginning of globalization as Asian nations started competing in world markets alongside countries from North America and Europe.

Capitalism Sweeps Asia

South Korea later began making high-quality electronics and automobiles in head-to-head competition with Japan. Then their huge neighbor, China, opened up its economy, effectively throwing hundreds of millions of low-paid workers into world markets. This reawakened a knack for commerce in Chinese culture that went back thousands of years. American companies, like Apple Computer, could now take advantage of the flexibility afforded by China's primitive agricultural sector (chapter 1).[1] Also, China's Communist party provided the top-down management style that mimicked that of successful Western corporations. Businessmen have always preferred dealing with dictators, kings, and generals. Democracy often injects uncertainty, and therefore increased risk, into business.*

India, another large, highly populated country, entered the global economy with certain built-in advantages. Since so many Indians spoke English, it was easy for them to interact directly with Western countries and their customers. While the proportion of educated, technically trained workers is much smaller than that in the United States or Europe, in absolute numbers, India has plenty of engineers, scientists, computer specialists, and managers out of its one-billion-plus population to start competing with the West. Indian culture has always valued higher education so the country's economic success further encouraged millions to go to school. Perhaps one day these young people would have an impact on the world similar to that of America's highly educated baby boomers.

These large Asian economies were not without their problems. China's undervalued currency makes its exports cheaper but produces domestic inflation and the possibility of societal unrest. Additionally, China has

---

* Businessmen want to control everything themselves, of course. That's why they have such a knee-jerk reaction against government regulation. But if they can exert enough control of Congress, then government restrictions may be better than the chaos of markets. This view can be seen in the careers of two of the most prominent figures in American capitalism, John D. Rockefeller and J. Pierpont Morgan. See Ron Chernow, *Titan* (New York: Random House, 1998) and Ron Chernow, *The House of Morgan* (New York: Simon & Schuster, 1990).

had to invest heavily in infrastructure to catch up with the West. India's stifling government bureaucracy makes it difficult to do business there. Japan has an aging population. It also suffered a severe economic downturn after a real estate bubble in the 1990s from which it has never fully recovered.

The economic crisis in the West, which started in the United States in 2007, has hurt many countries dependent on exports. Huge numbers of Asian workers are now employed in manufacturing, transportation, communications, and other areas in jobs far away from their homes in farms and villages. Their jobs have removed them from the direct production of necessities, a process described in chapters 1 thru 4 that has long been part of human economic development. These workers are now dependent on industrial jobs in the global economy.

Over thousands of years, the agricultural sector has shrunk from 100 percent of the work force to less than 3 percent in some advanced nations. However, Asian agriculture is not that efficient. Some industrial workers will still be needed in the farms and rice paddies but will commute to work in cities as needed. They offer flexibility in industrial employment that is lacking in the West.

Across Asia, hundreds of millions of people have achieved lifestyles that Americans would recognize as middle class or better. These Asian workers expect better housing, cars, medical care, vacations and leisure time, and improved diets with more protein. Luxury goods are in great demand. More and more people in Asia hope to enjoy Western-style consumption. How are you going to keep them down on the farm after they've seen Gucci, or

Versace, or Mercedes, or tasted Godiva chocolate? Global competition will only intensify as vast numbers of now low-paid workers improve their skills in order to compete for jobs that afford a higher standard of living.

The European Economic Community

The European Economic Community (EEC) was created to facilitate free trade by opening borders and eliminating bureaucratic restrictions. It was also meant to end a long history of conflicts in Europe. For example, the continent's two strongest countries, Germany and France, had often been at odds. (A language with no vowels cannot easily coexist peacefully next to a language with no consonants.) The EEC would relieve tensions across Europe by encouraging increased trade and other interactions between member countries.

The Eurozone is made up of countries in the EEC which use the euro as a common currency. The United Kingdom is an example of an EEC country that is not in the Eurozone. Problems arose because Eurozone status seemed to confer automatic credit-worthiness, which some countries and private borrowers took advantage of to get loans beyond their capacity to repay.

The normal remedy in this case for a "stand-alone" country would be to devalue its currency. This could be viewed as a natural market process, since the country's debtor status lowers the value of its output, assets, and labor. A devalued currency would reduce its imports by making them more expensive. It would also make its exports cheaper. The more favorable trade balance that resulted would allow it to pay off its debts. But with all

Eurozone countries using the same currency, single-country devaluation is not possible. Thus nations with severe debt problems like Greece and Italy could only either impose austerity measures or ask for at least partial debt forgiveness.

Austerity causes social unrest, while forgiving debts causes resentment among more responsible Eurozone members. Both remedies tend to reduce economic activity. Countries cannot shrink their way to growth, and ultimately economic growth is needed for recovery. The United States has a keen interest in the resolution of the Eurozone debt crisis because American banks hold European debt and because these countries are important trading partners.

The economic crisis in Europe and America offered two lessons: (1) financial regulations must be imposed on the private sector to prevent profit-seeking behavior that could destroy a national economy, and (2) countries must exercise prudent spending practices and maintain adequate levels of taxation to keep national debt from getting out of hand. The benefits of borrowed money and the joy of getting tax cuts delay the realization that fiscal policy may be irresponsible. Only the prospect of financial pain constrains people to rational behavior.

Plutocracy

In many countries of the world, mal-distribution of wealth gives a handful of people control of both the government and the economy. For centuries, this plutocratic model has described Latin American countries. They typically have low consumer demand and therefore low output despite abundant resources. There is relatively little national consumption, since most money goes to the wealthy. Additionally, rich people in these countries easily evade taxes since they influence law enforcement. Argentina has been a classic example of a plutocracy. Like the United States, it has plenty of natural resources, a favorable climate, abundant agricultural output, and lots of talented people from many years of immigration. But most wealth has flowed to the top, putting too much money in the hands of people with a low marginal propensity to consume (chapter 12).

Historically, Mexico has suffered from mal-distribution of income and wealth. For many years, Mexicans have had to go north to the United States to find work due to a lack of job opportunities in their homeland. For decades, the main growth industry in Mexico has been illegal drug activity, which has turned the country into a virtual narco-state. Though this is a morally reprehensible business, from a market point of view, drug dealers are simply entrepreneurs supplying demand in the United States while creating wealth and providing jobs. This increases consumption of all kinds on both sides of the border.

It is important for Americans to understand the plutocratic model because of the dramatic trend in the United States to ever-increasing mal-distribution of income and wealth. Based on the many experiences of Latin American countries, this mal-distribution will tend to choke off economic activity, increase unemployment, reduce democracy, and encourage social unrest. Ironically, these problems may eventually drive illegal immigrants away from the United States as they go south across the border to seek better job opportunities.

Brazil, a large, resource-rich, and increasingly democratic country, has prospered in recent years. Brazil's success gives hope that other Latin American countries, and even Middle Eastern and African countries, can begin to compete in the world economy. Global competition is not going away. Achievement of the American Dream now requires Americans to compete with people all over the world. Neither technology nor innovation will change that fact. Aside from laws barring exports of sensitive defense and intelligence technology, any innovation in the United States can be exported to take advantage of cheaper, yet qualified, labor elsewhere.

Apple Computer has created numerous products that stand out as examples of American ingenuity. While these products provide a large net economic benefit to the United States, most of the labor and raw materials used in their manufacture and distribution are from other countries. To retain as much employment as possible, the United States must continuously invest in the education, training, and infrastructure improvements necessary to maintain and enhance the American labor productivity that historically has given the United States a huge advantage over other countries.

Chapter 27
Economic Optimization

Hunting and gathering is the most natural economic system. A person wakes up in the morning and seeks necessities. But many centuries of economic development have created advanced industrial economies where people must have jobs to make money in order to buy things. Most people work in jobs that produce goods or services that are either optional or deferrable. A country with a functioning domestic economy and something to offer the world can be prosperous enough to support this fragile structure of easily eliminated jobs. "Something to offer the world" describes a comparative advantage—perhaps cheaper labor or mineral or agricultural resources—that earns money in world markets.

With many more affluent people and a larger population in the world, there has been an unprecedented demand for most of the world's resources, including food, minerals, energy, and even water. Will limited resources and an abundance of labor produce a zero-sum global economy with winners and losers? Will there be a negative-sum global economy with more losers than winners? Or can almost every advanced economy prosper?

Developing countries will, by definition, experience improvements, even with some bumps along the way. Many poor countries will remain poor. The historically advanced nations in North America and Europe will be most affected by globalization. For centuries they have had advantages over less-developed countries in the world, many of which were seen as nothing more than places and people to be exploited. The competitive global economy has changed much of that.

Maintaining Employment

For historically advanced countries, the fundamental economic problem of the twenty-first century will be how to maintain and create enough useful jobs. Of course, this will require countries to make investments in people, business, infrastructure, and research in order to compete in the global economy. Jobs cannot be taken for granted; they must be cultivated. A farmer does not just gaze out at his fields, waiting for the invisible hand of markets to make crops. The farmer takes action. Similarly, a country must actively create and pay for useful public sector jobs if the private sector cannot provide enough of them.

However, there is no reason to believe that the private sector will provide enough jobs. In addition to global competition and ever-increasing efficiency, the financial sector is a problem. Recall that Say's Law (chapter 15) was easily refuted by observing that the demands of money recipients in the economy need not match the output created. Money could simply be saved or even spent outside of the economy. For years, increased financial investments by wealthy people making ever higher incomes (chapter 9) have diminished any neat flow of money back into the real economy. For better or worse, any large accumulation of money with no place to go in the real economy will reside in the financial sector and this money may actually cause problems in the real economy. Earnings by Middle East oil exporters, now some $500 billion a year,[1] have been an indirect source of funding for the deficit spending and irresponsible lending practices in the United States and Europe that have cost many people their jobs.

Restoring a Healthy Economy

In a healthy economy, consumers spend money that they earn from jobs. This produces profits for businesses, creates new jobs, and spurs economic investment. Businesses respond to consumer demand. (People without jobs have no money to respond to supply.) There is a circular flow of money to businesses (for consumption of private sector output) and to government (for taxes to pay for public sector services), and then back to workers, suppliers, and contractors. Anything that disrupts this circular flow will reduce economic activity.

But a bizarre side effect of a market economy is the possibility that some people could receive huge, even ridiculous, levels of compensation. A single person might get hundreds of times the median national income. Since high-income people spend proportionally less than ordinary people (chapter 12), this threatens the circular flow of money in the economy. Of course, the problem is worsened by tax cuts for high earners. Anything that reduces overall consumption also diminishes economic investment opportunities.

The tax cuts in the United States in the early 1960s are often cited as evidence that reductions in high marginal tax rates will spur economic activity but any growth after these tax reductions was undoubtedly coincidental. It likely resulted from a general spirit of optimism in the country, combined with residual post-war consumer demand and the influx of the baby boomers (chapter 16). It is much more significant that even after the tax cuts, the highest marginal tax rates were 70 percent or more.[2] This allowed adequate circulation of money in the economy, which kept consumption and employment at healthy levels. Excessive wealth accumulation could have choked off economic activity. The same argument that refutes Say's Law also refutes the notion that tax cuts for the rich are necessarily good for the economy. There has never, ever been a reason to believe that tax cuts that excessively favor wealthy Americans will do anything but stifle economic activity.

Free markets will eventually adjust to any disruptions: war, disease, natural disasters, and even human stupidity. Sloppy mortgage lending practices in the United States from 2002 to 2006 (chapter 24) and excessive borrowing in the Eurozone (chapter 26) were easily accommodated by economic contractions. Reduced output, higher unemployment, hunger, and poverty are all just part of the market's adjustment to a new state of economic reality. If the United States had 20 percent unemployment, store shelves would be even easier to fill with an adequate supply of goods due to reduced consumer demand.

Like the speed of light in physics, the invisible hand in economics is always comfortably constant and predictable. In destitute areas in the Horn of Africa, the invisible hand brings the lack of effective economic demand for

Economic Optimization

food by starving populations into zero equilibrium with a lack of food supply. Only redistributive forces—charities, churches, and other countries—interrupt the market and feed people.

A free-market economy always works to move toward a neat equilibrium of supply and demand but the presence of human beings in the economy can spoil this. People tend to want food and other necessities, along with the jobs that allow them to buy these things. In a world that does not need everybody to work, it will always be necessary to combine the wealth creation of the distributive, capitalistic economic system with the redistributive functions of government (chapter 19) to optimize the level of economic activity.

In the 1980s, the economy was interrupted by policies that included arbitrarily cutting taxes and not paying the bills. It should be possible, in today's economy, to raise taxes in order to reduce high concentrations of money used for low rates of consumption and little economic investment and shift the money to better alternative uses in public goods and services. In particular, increased spending on public infrastructure and further support for education and training will create useful jobs while making the United States even more competitive in the global economy. Additionally, history has shown us that government investment in research has paid off handsomely for all Americans.

All of these "public investments" will enhance the circular flow of money and expand economic activity while producing more jobs, more consumption, increased business profits, more economic investment, and even additional tax revenue. People who are actually producers will benefit from these policies. Those who are merely acquirers of money will not. Economic optimization is the process of using progressive income taxation to expand economic activity and reduce debt while providing for needs that can only be satisfied by government.

The sluggish recovery following the Great Recession of 2007–09 is the direct result of misguided policies since 1981 that have encouraged mal-distribution of income and wealth and have over-rewarded people who do not proportionally contribute to consumption. On June 24, 2013, an Associated Press article, "Rising wealth not matched by spending," provided insight into the problem. Economist Edward Wolff of New York University calculated that the nation's median household net worth is only $61,000.* This is still 47 percent below where it was in 2007. However, wealthy Americans skew the mean household net worth to $522,000. Wolff said that these wealthy households save a lot of money while spending only a small proportion on basics like food and clothing.[3]

As we mentioned earlier, high-income people were taxed at marginal rates ranging from 70 percent to 90 percent during some of the most prosperous years in American history. Unlike in the 1950s and 1960s, the current low rates of taxation on high personal income do not allow sufficient redistribution of money for a healthy economy. This partially explains the lingering high unemployment after the Great Recession. It is not harmless

---

* Half of all households have a net worth below the median of $61,000 and half have a net worth greater than $61,000.

activity to construct public policy around the notion that rich people must constantly be given tax cuts. While the post-World War II era was peculiar in many ways (chapter 16), the economic optimization policy recommended here is just the name given to policies that worked before to produce prosperity.

Chapter 28
The Politics of Economics in America

Almost every law or government action has economic implications. Programs have costs; regulations restrict private sector activity. Politics in America is a debate about whether or not government should act based on cost-benefit analysis of issues by groups of people with differing ideological perspectives. No one would suggest that government do everything. Communal living invariably fails, except on the smallest scale. Some people oppose all taxation and therefore advocate virtually no government. Unfortunately, there is no twelve-step program for sociopathy.

Responsible conservatives insist on a strong military, homeland security, police and fire protection, courts and prisons to lock up the bad guys, roads and bridges, and the provision of at least some public health and education. These things, along with maintaining the basic functions of the three branches of government, guarantee that even in the most minimal conservative scenario, Americans will have "big government." The failure of the marketplace to provide certain necessities, such as flood insurance in flood-prone areas and primary health insurance for sick and dying old people, further expands the role of government in society.

Government functions will always be with us and they cannot easily be compared to private sector activity. These public functions exist precisely because they are either not provided by the private sector or because people do not want a profit motive to affect them. Getting a traffic ticket, fighting in the military, serving on a jury, and being forced to renew one's driver's license will never be like getting a manicure or buying a shirt. We don't want private sector police officers arresting more people just to increase police stock options.

Government activity is often the opposite of what we experience in the private sector. We are free to choose to buy furniture, but we are required to pay property taxes. In the private sector, spending is determined by income. With government, voters choose through their elected representatives to spend money and this determines how much income (tax revenue) government will need.

There is no preordained "correct" level of taxation. Taxes are determined by decisions to spend money. A decision to go to war is a decision to pay for war. Unless there is a timely spending reduction in some other area, taxes should increase automatically to pay for new expenditures. Otherwise, debt financing will obscure the public's responsibilities and deter rational fiscal policies. Even worse, bribing people with tax cuts in order to get their votes will certainly ensure fiscal disaster.

Public outcry for federal assistance after the monstrous 1927 Mississippi River flood (chapter 16) set precedence for the use of government intervention to solve large non-defense problems. There is no constitutional reason that Americans cannot provide each other with government assistance via well-established democratic processes. Indeed, the willingness and ability of citizens to use government to provide necessities unobtainable from the private sector may define the difference between a nation and a group of people who just happen to be living in the same part of the world.

Desperate Americans welcomed government programs by Democratic President Franklin Roosevelt in the Great Depression. Social Security would become the most successful social program in history, providing at least some minimal level of income to senior citizens and others while relieving their families and communities of a huge financial burden. Federal intervention was also used to correct societal injustices such as racism and widespread hunger. Exposing state and local problems to national and even international scrutiny had a huge impact on America. In the civil rights era, barbaric statements that got people reelected to state offices did not play well on a larger stage. Without federal intervention, there might still be legalized racial segregation in parts of the United States today. Even now, the inadequacies of some popular state political figures are exposed when they run for national office.

Anti-government Ideology

The Republican Party was dominant from 1860 to 1930,[1] but its opposition to FDR's policies during the Great Depression left the party out of step with most Americans. People couldn't eat anti-government, free-market rhetoric; they wanted food. In the 1964 presidential election, Republican senator Barry Goldwater ran on a theme opposing big government, socialism, and communism. He lost by a landslide to Lyndon B. Johnson who received 64 percent of the votes outside the South. There weren't many black voters in the South, and white voters there had switched to the Republican Party because of the Democrats' support of civil rights. In a period of optimism and prosperity before the war in Vietnam and the OPEC oil embargo, Americans widely supported Johnson's Great Society programs. Medicare, an irreplaceable health insurance program for older people was especially important. It was opposition to Johnson's war policies, not to his social programs, that caused LBJ to decline to run for reelection in 1968.

Democrats were emboldened by the success and acceptance of their government programs and perhaps got carried away at times. Not every problem can be solved by government and somebody has to pay for everything. Outlawing Happy Meal toys at McDonald's may be going too far. But if a law is not unconstitutional, then in the American system of government, it is a truism that decisions by the people's duly-elected representatives are the will of the people.

Philosophical objection to Americans' using government to help other Americans did not work for Republicans during the Great Depression. They needed to do something different and the economic misery of the 1970s (chapter 17) provided an opportunity. By 1980, Americans were ready for someone to promise them a return to the Age of Delusion. Many refused to believe that puny external forces like OPEC, Japan, Iran, or the Viet Cong could interfere with America's dominant military and economic position in the world. There had to be some insidious internal force working against them.

Ronald Reagan convinced many Americans that the enemy was the American government—the government of the people, by the people, and for the people. Republicans would enlist free-market advocates as allies. Ardent proponents of free-market capitalism tend to oppose government, particularly government regulation in the marketplace. They have not been deterred in this belief over the years despite the persistent failures of deregulation, especially in financial markets. The resulting high costs of inadequate regulation to the American people have made the expression "unregulated free markets" an oxymoron.

Social conservatives became another important ally. They could be counted on to vote based entirely on their beliefs on a few issues, even against candidates with whom they overwhelmingly agreed otherwise. Like clockwork, before each election Republicans would revive controversies over abortion rights, gay marriage, and public displays of religious items.

Conservatives' initial concerns about societal unrest and government interventions in the market (chapter 19) gave way to concerns about demographics. Conservatives didn't want to pay for the problems of increasing numbers of poor people, illegal immigrants, seniors in deteriorating health, "welfare mothers," liberals, and groups such as Hispanics and blacks that had less income and education than the general population. Hispanics were seen as a particular problem, since they were the fastest-growing segment of the American population. Increasingly, frustrated conservatives looked around them at the American people, didn't like what they saw, and didn't want to pay for it.

Anti-government Strategies

Changing demographics meant that time was not on the side of conservatives. They pursued remedies with anger and fierce intensity. Free-market beliefs and social issues were just tools, as were tax cuts. Later generations of Republicans would use Reagan's tax policies as a form of class warfare designed to cripple government and force the elimination of social programs which benefitted disfavored groups. Other effective tools included: forcing minority rule by requiring supermajorities in Congress before a vote could be taken, maintaining a Supreme Court majority, and restricting voting rights among certain people by any means necessary. Persistently ridiculing all government programs and their supporters was also effective. The predictable strains of an aging population on Medicare and Social Security budgets made these programs easy to attack.

Tax cuts disproportionately benefitting the rich diminished the important redistributive function of government that is necessary to maintain a healthy circular flow of money, especially in economic downturns (chapter 27). The United States suffered no ill effects from Reagan's tax cuts for twenty years since they were often offset by tax increases to reduce budget deficits. The market-driven collapse of oil prices in the mid-1980s revived the economy. In addition, the Reagan administration saw no major wars, George H.W. Bush exercised restraint in the 1991 Gulf War (chapter 20), and Bill Clinton benefited from the dot-com boom (chapter 21). But the huge economic crisis that began in the George W. Bush administration and continued for many years afterwards could be traced to a combination of tax cuts, inadequate financial regulation, and increased demand for government services. The Bush recession had the effect of impoverishing many more Americans, which further increased the need for government services.

Democrats often seem to be swamped by Republican rhetoric. They have no simplistic rebuttal to the Republicans' simplistic opposition to government. Republicans are inherently a minority party but their sense of desperation makes them very effective politically. Democrats represent the majority view on most domestic issues like Medicare and Social Security, but they are sometimes woefully ineffective as a political party. Democrats are able to consistently get 45 to 55 percent of the votes in national elections only because they represent the views of 60 to 70 percent of the American people on social programs.

Gerrymandered congressional districts created for political advantage at the state level have resulted in one-party elections that encourage extremism. This has produced a stalemate in a Congress filled with ideologues uninterested in making democracy work. The United States cannot move forward unless the underlying problem is corrected and there is no question where the problem lies. In the American system of government, there is no "they" in Washington to blame; there are only the officials elected by the voters. However, the country cannot afford to wait for today's voters to die off so that functioning government can be restored. People need to elect officials who will encourage the sacrifices necessary to pay the bills and revive the economy.

Chapter 29
Pay the Bills

In the competitive global economy, no country is in a better position to prosper than the United States of America. It has skilled workers, pervasive infrastructure, creative talent, and capital equipment in place. But it has huge economic problems, like high unemployment and a large national debt, and it has a political system seemingly unable to function. A lack of viable solutions to its problems calls into question whether Americans even understand the concept of a "problem." We may define a problem as an adverse circumstance whose correction requires sacrifice. The need for sacrifice is a critical part of the definition. If obesity could be corrected by eating ice cream, cake, and candy, then obesity would not be a problem; it would be an opportunity. But correcting obesity requires changes in eating habits, exercise, and maybe even surgery. These are all sacrifices.

We should be wary if someone tells us that a problem can be solved without sacrifice. Remember the old adage: "if it sounds too good to be true, then it probably is." We cannot increase retirement savings by putting money into high-return, risk-free investments. They don't exist. All we can do is save more money. We cannot pay mounting bills by working less and reducing our income. We need to work more and make extra money. We cannot pay off the national debt and pay for government services by cutting taxes and thus reducing the money available to pay off the national debt and pay for government services.

Less Tax but More Government

After 9/11, there was a huge increase in spending for homeland security and fighting wars in Afghanistan and Iraq. Then the collapse of the financial markets in 2007–08 put many Americans in need of assistance. Combine all of this with predictable demands on government for disaster relief, an aging population, and repaying debt, and it was clear that Americans could only solve these financial problems with sacrifices in the form of tax payments. Instead, the 2001 tax cuts were extended. No attempt was made to pay the bills. Tax revenues fell below the rate necessary to sustain a great nation. Former Republican senator Allen Simpson, co-chair of the Deficit Reduction Committee, said in August 2011 that "revenue coming into the US (government) is 15 percent of GDP, which is the lowest since the Korean War." The post-World War II average is 19.5 percent.[1] Though the percentage rose as the economy began to improve in 2012, low rates of taxation, combined with massive increases in demand for government services after 2000, significantly increased the nation's debt.

Inadequate taxation is not the only cause of America's economic crisis. High unemployment and lingering problems in the real estate markets in some parts of the country remind people of the continuing impact of the 2007–08 collapse in the mortgage industry (chapter 23). Big mistakes can cause big problems and it is not the case that every problem has a quick and easy solution. If a pedestrian gets hit by a speeding truck and survives, there is no upside, and recovery may take many years. The impact of the mortgage crisis will be with Americans for many years also. So will the economic destruction caused by years of misguided tax policies that largely favored wealthy people. By 2011, banks were awash in cash that had no place to go.[2] Rich people had more money than they needed for consumption, and neither the banks nor their depositors could find any economic investment opportunities in a down economy. Money just sat in the financial sector and outside of any circular flow of economic activity.

For several years after the mortgage crisis began in 2007, there were signs of "the negative multiplier effect" described in chapter 5 in which large numbers of economic decisions based quite sensibly on self-interest combined to make the economy worse. In a steep abnormal downturn with domestic causes (chapter 15), there is a danger that a market economy will implode. A study by two former Census Bureau officials reported in October 2011 that income levels had been falling since December 2007.[3] In September 2011, the Census Bureau itself indicated that the poverty level was at a near twenty-year high.[4] The US workforce shrunk by 529,000 people from November 2010 to April 2011 as workers became discouraged by lack of employment opportunities.[5] The labor force participation rate of 64.2 percent was the lowest since 1984. And people were exhausting their employment benefits, so that by November 2011, only 48 percent of the unemployed were getting benefits, down from 75 percent in early 2010.[6] The US economy had been hit by several trucks, including a lack of adequate financial regulation and increased spending combined with reduced tax revenue.

By 2012, improvements in the housing markets,

booming activity in oil and gas drilling, and a rising stock market, were all causes for optimism. Consumer confidence was slowly increasing and unemployment was gradually decreasing. But the level of taxation was still inadequate to meet the demand for government services and to pay off the national debt that had accumulated since the beginning of the Great Recession.

More taxes are not the only answer. All government expenditures should be reviewed for possible savings. But people will not stop getting old, and old people will not stop getting sick. Children will not educate themselves. Eighty-year-old infrastructure designed to last fifty years will continue to deteriorate. Foreign enemies will not unilaterally surrender. Natural disasters will not stop occurring. Hungry people cannot eat self-serving political rhetoric. A critically important problem is that any reduction in government spending that eliminates jobs or reduces payments to recipients of government money (e.g., the military, government contractors, retirees, and "welfare mothers") will make the economy worse by reducing consumption, thus hurting business. There is a reason economics is called "the dismal science." It often seems that for every policy advantage there is a corresponding disadvantage.

But something has to be done. Most proposals to cut government spending suggest ways to save, say, $1 trillion over ten years. But with a $17 trillion deficit, $100 billion per year in savings is insignificant if, in addition to interest payments, additional tax cuts add to the debt. Solving big problems requires big sacrifices. Fairness to future generations requires that the Americans who spent the money should be the ones to pay the bills.

The military has fought bravely for years, with many Americans in uniform sustaining injuries or worse. Now it is time for civilians to do their part in protecting America. The people of the United States must break the chains of ideology, roll up their sleeves, and pay the bills with the same sense of obligation and patriotism that Americans on the home front exhibited in World War II. Cutting out waste and inefficiency is always in order but that is not enough. To revive the economy, money must be shifted to people who will use it for consumption.

Revive the Economy and Pay the Bills

Here are specific recommendations with the rationale behind them. Some combination of these suggestions would raise enough money to win the war on the national debt, restore a healthy circular flow of money to increase economic activity, and create jobs:

- Eliminate most of the George W. Bush tax cuts. This reduction in revenue during a time of increased spending never made any sense. Add a marginal tier of taxes at 50 percent for those making $300,000 or more per year and a tier at 60 percent for those making $1 million or more. These proposals will go a long way toward correcting past mistakes.
- Raise capital gains tax rates. Some small long-term capital gain rate advantage could be retained to provide market stability but there is no reason that this particular kind of income should get preferential treatment over earned income. Employees and business owners who actually make a company money shouldn't have to pay taxes at higher marginal

rates than people who simply buy something and sit on it for a year or more before selling it.

- Increase federal fuel taxes by fifty cents a gallon. This regressive tax will reduce oil imports and encourage the use of more efficient forms of transportation. The new tax receipts can be spread among debt reduction, infrastructure, education, Medicare, and Social Security. People who continue to use lots of gasoline will be doing their patriotic duty to get the country out of a crippling economic bind. Those who conserve fuel will help reduce payments for oil imports.

- Tax recipients of inheritance at ordinary rates (in addition to the existing estate tax) on any inheritance above $6 million, adjusted for inflation each year, with higher exemptions available for heirs with physical or mental problems. This would tend to distribute great inheritance to a larger number of heirs, thus increasing consumption spending.

- Use a substantial part of any new tax revenue to pay down the national debt. This could be done at a rate much faster than with any previous proposals.

- Use increased infrastructure repairs and construction to provide new jobs in every state, converting idle Americans to working consumers and taxpayers.

- Make public education a growth industry through increased spending. This would repeat the success of the 1960s and 1970s with the baby boomers. There should be special emphasis on preparing people to do the high-value-added jobs that will make them competitive in the global economy. High institutional standards should be introduced for both college education and vocational training as criteria for giving students Department of Education loans. This would eliminate the current proliferation of for-profit pseudo-educational businesses whose main purpose is to get people to borrow money for "tuition" to fund profits and marketing expenses. The country should offer more full scholarships at legitimate educational institutions, based on student achievement and need. This would help alleviate the impact of reduced state funding of higher education that has resulted from the widespread attack on government and taxation since 1981. Universal pre-K education would produce a dramatic improvement in the nation's education system. It would take advantage of the natural receptiveness to learning by three- and four-year-old children and would help identify health and learning problems early. Additionally, funding research at colleges and universities has already led to new products in such fields as medicine, energy, and digital technology, and additional research funding may one day lead to the next great economic boom.

- Do not require Medicare Advantage programs to offer any extra benefits but, at the same time, give no greater reimbursement to these private plans than that for traditional Medicare. Increase Medicare payments and reduce patient co-pays to primary care physicians and nurse practitioners in order to encourage people to seek medical care at the most economical level possible.

- Fund a voluntary, nationwide public service program which would allow people to work in their communities. This would be especially useful for newly discharged veterans and young people who have not yet successfully entered the workforce. It could be combined with part-time college study or vocational training. Volunteers could clean up after natural disasters, tutor younger students, or build housing for low-income families.
- Give foreign graduate students an opportunity to demonstrate their business skills after they receive their degrees, and encourage those who can contribute to the economy to stay in the United States. Recruit successful high-income people from all over the world to come to the United States to live and do business. There are Chinese millionaires who would prefer the freedom in America.[7] Already, wealthy Mexicans flock to Texas with their families to escape the drug wars south of the border. In effect, the United States can reap the rewards for letting others share in America's freedoms. Perhaps one day, Americans themselves will be willing to pay for the advantages their country has to offer.

There will be loud and intense opposition to the above suggestions. However, these suggestions are meant to shift money from high-income people with low rates of consumption to activities that satisfy unmet needs while encouraging more consumption, increased employment, more economic investment, and a healthier economy. Multi-billionaire investor Warren Buffett is known for his sensible approach to financial matters.

When he suggested that wealthy people like himself should be taxed at a higher rate, he was rebuked by some members of Congress.[8] Thirty-plus years of continuous ideological impairment have left many prominent politicians in the United States unable to grasp the concept of using tax revenue to pay for government expenditures demanded by the American people.

Chapter 30
One Nation, Divisible

Huge mistakes, like inadequate financial regulation and years of tax cuts in the face of increased demand for essential government services, have created big problems that require the sacrifices necessary for big solutions. The economy could be revived by widespread job creation in education and infrastructure combined with already strong activity in the medical and energy sectors. Sacrifices would be rewarded by increased employment, reduced national debt, and greater prosperity. Wealthy Americans would pay more money than others but would suffer virtually no loss of satisfaction (chapter 12). Shifting money from those who spend proportionally little to retirees and lower- and middle-income Americans who spend almost every dollar they get, will increase overall consumption and spur business activity. Pent-up consumer demand by people who had been unemployed or underemployed would increase spending.

Defining a Nation
Realistically, a people who have been persistently rewarded for supporting irresponsible fiscal policies are not likely to accept the need for sacrifice. They have been told that self-interest is all that matters. But what about the country? Is America nothing more than just collateral damage to policies based on extremist political and economic ideology? Can such a diverse collection of human beings unite to do anything?

Currently, the United States just barely meets the minimum requirements to be a nation. It has political subdivisions: federal, state, county, and municipal. There are administrative departments within these political subdivisions. But Americans are not united by their history, which has often been one of conflict. Nor are they united by their laws or their constitution. These are like the rules of baseball, which simply define the terms under which teams differ and compete.

There are two things necessary to define a nation. One is the willingness to come together and solve big problems, such as the Great Depression, World War II, and the economic downturn that started at the end of 2007. The other is the ability to set aside narrow self-interests, act in good faith, and recognize that it is always easier to impede and even destroy democratic processes than it is to make them work. There is no place in a democratic government for bizarre economic theories or elected officials committed to obstructing the will of the people. It is important that government provide necessities unavailable elsewhere and that these services are paid for in a timely manner.

Misconception Behind Public Policies

Too often public policies are based on false or outdated premises:
- "Government is bad. The market is good." But we are still waiting for the market's response to the December, 1941, Pearl Harbor attack. Without government there would be no national defense or police protection or Medicare or homeland security.

- "Things should be like the 1950s and 1960s when the American Dream was alive and well." But now, people all over the world are pursuing their own versions of the American Dream. No longer will very ordinary people, with nothing special to offer the world, and no particular education or training, be able to routinely achieve a middle-class lifestyle just because they were born in the USA. Sure, they work hard, but people all over the world work hard.
- "American ingenuity will save us." People are quick to take credit for the accomplishments of Thomas Edison, Henry Ford, and Steve Jobs. But at least 99.9 percent of Americans will never exhibit such ingenuity.
- "The United States is the greatest nation on earth." It is, and Americans should be willing to work and sacrifice to keep it that way. But the most critically needed entitlement reform is to get people to understand that prosperity is not a birthright—they must compete for it. Hundreds of millions of workers in other countries have tasted a middle-class lifestyle and have huge incentives to continue taking American jobs just as they have already done in computer programming, customer service, and textiles and other manufacturing industries.
- "Americans are financially well off and should expect to provide everything for themselves, including their future retirement and medical care." An overlooked observation by Charles Murray in his book *Losing Ground* was that "historically, the United States has been a nation of people who were either poor or

the children of poor parents. Only in the last half of the twentieth century has a large proportion of the middle class become so far removed from poverty that the lack of money became horrifying in itself."[1] Americans have had a distorted view of economics since the Age of Delusion (chapter 16). Now, a somewhat optimistic view of a typical American family would show that they have a net worth of about $80,000, with some of the money tied up in home equity and autos and not available for spending. They have no pension plan, and non-retirement savings are inadequate for any unexpected setbacks such as job loss or serious health problems. They use their resources to help their children but they may have difficulty accumulating enough in their lifetime to help any future grandchildren. They relax at public parks, not private clubs. Public schooling is their best opportunity for a better future. As they grow old, the lights at the end of the tunnel are Medicare and Social Security.

- "Americans are rugged individualists who grow crops and raise animals in order to be self-sufficient. They build their own log cabins, apply home remedies for health problems, and use horses for transportation." In fact, most Americans are dependent on other people for a job. Even self-employed Americans are dependent on their customers for income. Never in human history has it been more important to be part of a functional society. Roads, bridges, airports, public education, police and fire protection, and a safety net in case of a natural disaster, job loss, or disability; are all now essential to elevate people above the Darwinian world of our primitive ancestors.

Politicians and political parties are adept at taking advantage of busy people who spend little time learning about the issues of the day. Political platforms are marketed like consumer products. Just as the sales of poorly made vehicles can be increased with clever commercials, poor public policy can be promoted with attractive come-ons and catchy statements. Who wouldn't want to get more and pay less? And if people can be induced to go to war for no reason, then think how easy it is to market foolish economic policies that only produce casualties in the distant future.

Taking advantage of the difference between the truth and what people want to believe could be called "intellectual arbitrage." This difference can be created by offering an appealing alternative to the truth. Voters need to consider what is important over the course of their lives and the lives of future generations and they must insist on paying the bills in order to protect the country. Essential government services cannot be funded by debt while Americans devote their lives to giving tax cuts to the wealthy. That is truly the Road to Serfdom.

Final Thoughts

This book does not contradict any accepted economic theory. It presents fundamental topics in economics, finance, and history, and it also addresses two important areas of concern. One is the place in the economic world of that most neglected of variables: human beings. At issue is whether our understanding of economics and the policies derived from that understanding adequately accommodate people in their quest for work or other means to obtain necessities. Secondly, the book looks at the impact on America of policies derived from ideologies and on the political machinations that have been used to push those foolish policies. Anti-government ideology, in particular, has proven to be dangerous and has consistently failed since 1981.

Americans have a distorted view of economic reality because of the country's peculiar history, especially since World War II. For thousands of years, the world-wide trend in economic development has been toward greater efficiency and displacing workers who then go on to different jobs. This trend has tended to move people from producing necessities to working on optional goods and services. As a result, many jobs are easily dispensed with when the economy is slow. Job losses from increased efficiency began even before mechanization and computers were available to replace people, and also before professional managers appeared on the scene with monetary incentives to use less labor.

And now, other countries are eager to take American jobs and even entire American industries.

The world has never needed everyone to work and many jobs exist only because taxpayers reluctantly support them. In chapter 2, I gave a purely hypothetical example indicating that if there were no crime, the economy would have little need for the millions of people who, one way or the other, are provided for by the criminal justice system. Since 2011, the return to civilian life of soldiers who fought in the Middle East has provided us with an actual example that we may not need everyone to work.[1] These former soldiers joined civilians seeking jobs even as the soldiers' lost incomes and reduced purchasing power combined with the end of wartime spending to shrink both economic activity and the need for workers in the economy.

It is an example of the Fallacy of Composition to suggest that the solution to everyone's personal financial problem is simply for them to get a job. In a competitive world, there is no reason to believe that work will be available for everybody who needs a job. This is not an insignificant point considering that after air and water, other necessities are typically provided by money earned from work. This underlying economic reality has become more apparent now due to global competition, increased efficiency, and an economic downturn in some parts of the world. But where was this reality before? It was all around us. Throughout even the most prosperous periods in American history, there was always an underclass of people who did not work: the unskilled, people with chronic medical problems, the uneducated, and people who found themselves in economically depressed areas. No needed output went unproduced because of their inactivity. The economy only needed their consumption, not their labor.

During the Great Depression, agriculture was a very large part of the American economy. It was easy to just keep the unemployed on the family farms if their labor wasn't needed elsewhere. The Great Recession started in 2007, and its impact continues today with relatively high unemployment and a national debt crisis. But in twenty-first century America, few people have a family farm to go to, and the definition of "necessities" has expanded to include more and better health care, electronic communication, and readily available transportation. In the 1930s, just about any job would have paid for the minimal food, clothing, and shelter that were the standard necessities of the day. But now, a minimum-wage job is not adequate to provide the basic necessities of life.

A Lesson from the History of Physics

The realities of economics on a small scale (people's requirements for necessities and adequate jobs) and on a large scale (a country's place in the global economy) invite a comparison to the science of physics. The great English physicist Sir Isaac Newton (1642–1727)[2] gave a brilliant explanation of the physical world around us. His theories seemed to accommodate every practical application in science and engineering. But human beings are of a rather awkward size. They are too large to readily see the very small, subatomic world, but too small to easily understand the very large world of the cosmos. Human perception of reality proved to be incorrect. Newtonian physics was largely displaced by modern physics: Quantum Theory and the Theory of Relativity. These provided a more accurate but intuitively less obvious explanation of physical reality.

The social science of economics also has a history of relying on intuitively appealing but simplistic theories. Shared income in a redistributive system seems to accommodate the needs of everyone, but at the expense of less overall production on the larger (cosmological) economic scale. Lack of incentives stifles initiative and risk-taking, producing less aggregate output. But a distributive system that does offer incentives may neglect the individual (quantum) economic world of people who may struggle just to survive. In that world, very small events such as the need for auto repairs may produce a stark choice between maintaining transportation to work, or paying the rent but losing a job.

To take this imperfect analogy a step further, physicists studying the universe ask themselves how it could have developed in such a way to accommodate intelligent human beings like themselves. In his book, *A Brief History of Time*, noted physicist Stephen Hawking describes the "weak anthropic principle," which roughly states that in certain parts of the universe, conditions developed that allowed the existence of people who could be there asking questions about their existence.[3] Hawking further states that "it is a bit like a rich person living in a wealthy neighborhood not seeing any poverty." People's views are often determined by their own peculiar circumstances. The Fallacy of Composition (chapter 5) is universal.

Unlike the physical universe, the economic universe is rapidly changing with global competition and new demands on the world's resources. Americans have formed opinions based on the economic history that produced them, that of a resource-rich, largely self-contained country that immediately after World War II had no competition. There is no reason to believe that this view will match the economic reality of equilibrium output and wages determined by the global economy. Jobs are so important that a country cannot take a chance on the untested theory that in this global environment, free markets alone will produce adequate employment.

Free market theory has gained the status of a religion, often replacing Judeo-Christian principles as a guide to dealing with the needs and problems of human beings. Its commandment that government is bad threatens to impede certain large-scale cooperative activities that may be essential. Other commandments indicating that taxes and regulation are sinful have also done immense damage to the country. In my youth, the most extreme criticism of the American government came from external enemies, particularly Communist leaders and third-world dictators. Now the criticism comes from within. It seems to have started with certain Americans who claimed that their freedoms were somehow jeopardized, despite the fact that they lived in the freest country on earth. Their problems were properly the province of psychiatry, not economics, but their ideas were seized upon by certain politicians for their own purposes.

Rejecting Anti-American-Government Ideology

If this book seems to support government more than is currently fashionable, it is because the pendulum of public opinion has swung too far toward an anti-American-government sentiment. It is understandable that in a rapidly changing world that puts people under great stress and in a complex economy where the "American Dream" seems less obtainable than ever, people would look for a scapegoat. Voting for policies that increase the national debt and underfund important programs guarantees that government will disappoint us. It is disturbing that in a democratic country, people so readily complain about the government that they alone control.

Ever mindful of the Fallacy of Composition, I will describe a few of the complaints that I have heard about government:

- A fifty-year-old man has to be coerced into using his automobile seatbelt. Despite overwhelming evidence of its safety benefits, he resists because he argues that this represents government intrusion into his personal freedom.
- A saleswoman works at an auto dealership located at the intersection of two major highways. The dealership is located there because the heavy traffic gives it exposure to many potential customers. The heavy traffic also damages the highways. When the city government repairs and widens the road, it temporarily makes it difficult for people to get to her employer. She complains that this "government interference" in market activity is hurting her income.
- In 2001, tropical storm Allison produced massive

flooding in the Houston area, killing several people and devastating property. After a wealthy mega-church mechanically accumulated used clothing and other discarded items for the victims, its pastor complained that FEMA personnel were not readily available to receive the donations. Apparently, church members were eager to get rid of the stuff and hit the golf course, and they had no Christian sympathy for government employees who had to leave their families, travel hundreds of miles, and find housing in a city where hotels were filling up with flood evacuees, insurance adjustors, and outside media representatives.

- A self-employed taxpayer had taken a substantial deduction from his business income for car mileage. He falsely claimed tens of thousands of business miles on his tax return where he indicated that he had written records to justify this deduction. When the IRS asked that he send them photocopies of his mileage records, he complained that the government was intrusive.

- Several people complained about the PBS television network because it is partly supported by taxpayers. They argued, for example, that children's programming could be provided by commercial networks. But shows like *Sesame Street* were developed on public television because early commercial attempts at such programming had little to offer children. Those shows that were available commercially were often nothing more than a bunch of adults in costumes acting silly while trying to attract sponsors' money.

- An eighty-year-old widow is often complimentary about the ease and quality of the Medicare insurance coverage she receives. Without Medicare, she would have no health insurance. Without Social Security, she would have virtually no income. Yet she persistently agrees with, and votes for, politicians who tell her that government is bad.

The list could go on. Americans have been easy marks for anti-American-government extremists. Wrecking the government's finances by not paying the bills is intended to shrink or eliminate programs that the extremists oppose. Perversely, the extremists have benefited politically from this strategy even as the need and popularity of these programs have increased. In the 1940s and 1950s, investigators turned the country upside down looking for communists behind every bush. But that internal threat pales in comparison to the danger that the country now faces from the irresponsible fiscal policies and obstruction of government pushed by a vocal minority. Where is a congressional investigation when you really need one?

The American people can't have everything from government but they must have some things from government. Medicare, for example, is irreplaceable. And there is no reason that for-profit insurance companies should be allowed to make money from Medicare when they can't provide insurance in the usual way. Americans should be wary of any plans to shift Social Security money to private accounts in the financial sector. The choir boys on Wall Street are known to look out only for themselves. Family and friends of Social Security recipients cannot run the risk that people they know will lose these important retirement funds. Also, some government regulation will always be necessary. Opposing regulation is part of the job description of many business leaders. But it is to everybody's advantage to minimize tainted food, defective baby cribs, dangerous prescription drugs, and unsafe working conditions. Voters must avoid simplistic policies when deciding the proper role of government.

The American economy will continue to recover from the lingering effects of the Great Recession. The inherent strengths of the US economic system have already produced improvements. The concern is that, over time, more and more people will be left out of the economy. Rather than have these people dependent on charity, it is better to have government provide the necessary services and jobs that cannot come from the private sector. It is also important to prepare Americans to compete in the global economy. This will not be possible if voters allow the creation of a permanent structural defect in the nation's fiscal policy by restricting taxation to a level that is both insufficient to meet the needs of the people, and inadequate to sustain a great nation.

Endnotes

Part I
Chapter 1
[1] Jared Diamond, *Guns, Germs, and Steel* (New York: W.W. Norton & Co., 1997), 35.

Chapter 2
[1] Lauren E. Glazer, "Correctional Population of the United States, 2009," U.S. Department of Justice, Bureau of Correctional Statistics, December, 2010.

Part II
Chapter 5
[1] Douglas Brinkley, *The Great Deluge* (New York: Harper Collins, 2006), xiii.

Chapter 6
[1] Liaquat Ahamed, *Lords of Finance* (New York: Penguin Press, 2009), 430.

[2] Campbell R. McConnell, *Economics*, Fifth Edition (New York: McGraw-Hill Book Co., 1972), 302.

Chapter 8
[1] Interview with the real "Mrs. Smith," January, 1974.

[2] National Flood Insurance Act of 1968, FEMA website, accessed June 25, 2013, http://www.fema.gov/library/viewRecord.do?id=2216.

Chapter 9
[1] Andrew Ross Sorkin, *Too Big to Fail* (New York: Viking, 2009), 272.

Chapter 15
[1] Charles D. Cathcart, *Money, Credit, and Economic Activity* (Homewood, Illinois: Richard D. Irwin, Inc., 1982), 308.

[2] John D. Hicks, George E. Mowry, and Robert E. Burke, *The American Nation* (Boston: Houghton, Miffin Company, 1963), 543--545.

[3] Ingrid H. Rima, *Development of Economic Analysis* (Homewood, Illinois; Richard D. Irwin, Inc., 1967), 331.

[4] McConnell, *Economics*, 203.

Part III
Chapter 16
[1] Hicks, Mowry, and Burke, *The American Nation*, 256.

[2] Ibid., 110.

[3] Federal-Aid Highway Act of 1956, Federal Highway Administration website, accessed June 25, 2013, http://www.fhwa.dot.gov/publications/publicroads/96summer/p96su10.cfm.

Chapter 17
[1] Steve Fraser, *Wall Street: A Cultural History* (London: Faber and Faber, 2005), 473.

[2] James A. Clark and Michel T. Halbouty, *The Last Boom* (New York: Random House, 1972), 271.

[3] "Historic Crude Oil Prices, 1861 to Present," ChartsBin.com, accessed June 25, 2013, http://chartsbin.com/view/oau.

Chapter 18
[1] John Skow, "The Long Ordeal of the Hostages," January 26, 1981, *Time*, accessed June 15, 2011, http://www.time.com/time/magazine/article/0,9171,954605,00.html.

Part IV
Chapter 19
[1] Jay E. Greene, *100 Great Thinkers* (New York: Washington Square Press, 1967), 521–527.

[2] Milton Friedman and Rose Friedman, *Free to Choose* (New York: Harcourt Brace Jovanovich, 1979), 9–20.

[3] "Federal Individual Income Tax Rate History," Tax Foundation website, accessed June 15, 2011, www.taxfoundation.org.

Chapter 20
[1] *World Book Encyclopedia*, 11th ed., s.v. "World War II."

[2] C. L. Sulzberger, *The American Heritage Picture History of World War II*, (New York: American Heritage Publishing Company, Inc., 1966), 249–303.

[3] *World Book Encyclopedia*, 11th ed., s.v. "Korean War."

[4] *World Book Encyclopedia*, 11th ed., s.v. "Vietnam War."

[5] Thomas E. Ricks, *Fiasco: The American Military Adventure in Iraq*, (New York: The Penguin Press, 2006), 193.

[6] *World Book Encyclopedia*, 11th ed., s.v. "Afghanistan."

[7] *World Book Encyclopedia*, 11th ed., s.v. "Persian Gulf War, 1991."

[8] *World Book Encyclopedia*, 11th ed., s.v. "Afghanistan."

[9] *World Book Encyclopedia*, 11th ed., s.v. "US War in Iraq, 2003."

[10] Ricks, *Fiasco: The American Military Adventure in Iraq*, 15.

Chapter 21

[1] Gary Reback, *Free the Market* (New York: The Penguin Group, 2009), 33–45.

[2] Fraser, *Wall Street: A Cultural History*, 496.

[3] Timothy Curry and Lynn Shibut, "The Cost of the Savings and Loan Crisis: Truth and Consequences," FDIC Banker's Review website, accessed June 25, 2013, http://fdic.gov/bank/analytical/banking/2000dec/brv13n2_2.pdf.

[4] Norman Strunk and Fred Case, "When deregulation went wrong: a look at the causes behind savings and loan failures in the 1980s," United States Savings and Loan Institutions, 1988, 15–16.

[5] Fraser, *Wall Street: A Cultural History*, 495.

[6] "The Banking Crisis of the 1980s and early 1990s: Summary and Implications," FDIC website, accessed June 25, 2013, http://www.fdic.gov/bank/historical/history/3_85.pdf.

[7] Fraser, *Wall Street: A Cultural History*, 47.

[8] "Employment status of the civilian non-institutional population 16 years and over, 1940 to date," United States Bureau of Labor Statistics, accessed June 15, 2011, http://www.bls.gov/cps/prov_yrs.htm.

[9] Lou Cannon, *President Reagan: The Role of a Lifetime* (New York: Public Affairs, 2000), 235.

[10] Larry M. Bartels, "Constituency Opinion and Congressional Policy Making: The Reagan Defense Build Up," The American Political Science Review, 85 (2), January 1, 1991, 457–474.

[11] *World Book Encyclopedia*, 11th ed., s.v. "George H.W. Bush."

[12] "Bush, George Herbert Walker," archived from original MSN Encarta on October 31, 2009, archive copy at Wayback Machine, accessed January 11, 2012, http://encarta.msn.com/encyclopedia_761571000/George_H_W_Bush.html.

[13] *World Book Encyclopedia*, 11th ed., s.v. "William Jefferson Clinton."

Chapter 22

[1] *World Book Encyclopedia*, 11th ed., s.v. "George W. Bush".

[2] Dana Priest and William M. Arkin, "A hidden world, growing beyond control," *Washington Post* website, accessed October 11, 2011, http://projects.washingtonpost.com/top-secret-america/articles/a-hidden-world-growing-beyond-control/.

[3] Ricks, *Fiasco: The American Military Adventure in Iraq*, 145.

Chapter 23

[1] Sorkin, *Too Big to Fail*, 145.

[2] Chris Isidore, "Mortgage defaults: Latest woe for housing," CNN Money website, accessed June 15, 2011, http://money.cnn.com/2007/02/12/news/economy/subprime_realestate/index.htm.

[3] "US Foreclosure Activity Increases 75 Percent in 2007," Realtytrac website, accessed June 15, 2011, http://www.realtytrac.com/content/press-releases/us-foreclosure-activity-increases-75-percent-in-2007-3604.

[4] Sorkin, *Too Big to Fail*, 175.

[5] Ibid., 426.

[6] Ibid., 59.

[7] Ibid., 236.

[8] *Wall Street Journal* Blog; "Barney Frank Celebrates Free Market Day," September 17, 2008.

[9] Associated Press, "Census Housing Bust Worst Since Depression," *Houston Chronicle*, October 7, 2011.

[10] "Impact of Quantitative Easing on the Stock Market," MTPredictor website, accessed June 15, 2011, http://www.mtpredictor.us/1061/impact-of-quantitative-easing-on-the-stock-market/.

[11] "The Recession of 2007--2009," Bureau of Labor Statis-

tics website, accessed June 26, 2013, http://www.bls.gov/spotlight/2012/recession/pdf/recession_bls_spotlight.pdf.

[12] "Experts: Bush Presidency is a Failure, Little Chance to Improve Ranking," Sienna Research Institute website, accessed June 15, 2011, http://www.siena.edu/uploadedfiles/home/parents_and_community/community_page/sri/independent_research/Presidents%20Survey_06_may.pdf.

[13] Susan Page, "Disapproval of Bush Breaks Record," *USA Today*, accessed June 15, 2011, http://usatoday30.usatoday.com/news/washington/2008-04-21-bushrating_N.htm.

Chapter 24

[1] Sorkin, *Too Big to Fail*, 89.

[2] "The CRA and Subprime Lending: Discerning the Difference," Banking and Community Perspectives, Federal Reserve Bank of Dallas website, accessed June 26, 2013, http://www.dallasfed.org/assets/documents/cd/bcp/2009/bcp0901.pdf.

[3] Krishna Guha, Saskia Scholtes, and James Politi, "Saviors of the Suburbs," *Financial Times*, accessed June 15, 2011, http://www.ft.com/cms/s/0/c658585c-31d0-11dd-b77c-0000779fd2ac.html#axzz2XKrNTFdQ.

[4] Nelson D. Schwartz and Kevin Roose, "US sues major banks over risky investments," *Houston Chronicle*, September 3, 2011.

[5] Sorkin, *Too Big to Fail*, 230.

[6] Ben Rooney, "Fannie, Freddie got bailout--execs got big pay," CNN Money, accessed June 15, 2011, http://money.cnn.com/2011/04/01/news/companies/fannie_mae_freddie_mac_compensation/index.htm.

Chapter 25
[1] *World Book Encyclopedia*, 11th ed., s.v. "Barack Obama."

[2] Noam M. Levey, "US falls behind other nations in health care, report finds," *Houston Chronicle*, October 19, 2011.

[3] Edward Wyatt, "J.P. Morgan Chase, SEC settle," *Houston Chronicle*, June 22, 2011.

[4] David S. Hilzenrath, "SEC questions practices of credit rating agencies," *Houston Chronicle*, October 1, 2011.

[5] Carolyn Said, "California goes it alone on bank settlement talks," *Houston Chronicle*, October 1, 2011.

[6] "After Iraq exit, US will boost troops in Persian Gulf," *Houston Chronicle*, October 30, 2011.

Part IV
Chapter 26
[1] Charles Duhigg and Keith Bradsher, "For Apple, 'Made in USA' is a relic of a bygone era," *Houston Chronicle*, January 22, 2012.

Chapter 27
[1] Wayne Kelly and Richard S. Bishop, "Economic Limits to Oil Supply: a Non-Hubert Curve View," *Houston Geological Society Bulletin*, March 2011.

² "Federal Individual Income Tax Rate History," Tax Foundation website, accessed June 15, 2011, www.taxfoundation.org .

³ Associated Press, "Rising wealth not matched by spending," *Houston Chronicle*, June 24, 2013.

Chapter 28
¹ "The 1964 Presidential Election—Further Adventures in Wonderland," in Robert R. Jones and Gustav L. Seligmann, *The Sweep of American History* (New York: John Wiley & Sons, 1970), 54.

Chapter 29
¹ Belinda Luscombe, "Ten Questions," *Time*, August 8, 2011, 64.

² Eric Dash and Nelson D. Schwartz, "Banks flush with cash they can't use," *Houston Chronicle*, October 20, 2011.

³ Robert Pear, "Income levels are still falling," *Houston Chronicle*, October 10, 2011.

⁴ Jeanine Kever, "Poverty level near 20-year high," *Houston Chronicle*, September 14, 2011.

⁵ Associated Press, "A shrinking US workforce presents an economic puzzle," *Houston Chronicle*, June 3, 2011.

⁶ Associated Press, "Most US unemployed no longer get benefits," *Houston Chronicle*, November 7, 2011.

[7] Associated Press, "Top of Chinese wealthy's wish list? To Leave," *Houston Chronicle*, September 8, 2011.

[8] Ken Geiger, "Republicans beg to differ with Buffett," *Houston Chronicle*, August 17, 2011.

Chapter 30
[1] Murray, *Losing Ground*, 179.

Final Thoughts
[1] Shala Dewan, "Young vets return to home to scant work prospects," *Houston Chronicle*, December 18, 2011.

[2] Jay E. Greene, *100 Great Scientists* (New York: Washington Square Press, 1967), 112.

[3] Stephen Hawking, *A Brief History of Time* (Toronto: Bantam Books, 1988), 124–125.

Selected Bibliography

Ahamed, Liaquat. *Lords of Finance*. New York: Penguin Press, 2009.

Bach, George Leland. *Economics, Sixth Edition*. Englewood Clifts, New Jersey: Prentice-Hall, Inc., 1968.

Barry, John M. *Rising Tide*. New York: Simon & Schuster, 1997.

Brinkley, Douglas. *The Great Deluge*. New York: Harper Collins, 2006.

Cathcart, Charles D. *Money, Credit, and Economic Activity*. Homewood, Illinois: Richard D. Irwin, Inc., 1982.

Chernow, Ron. *The House of Morgan*. New York: Simon & Schuster, 1990.

Chernow, Ron. *Titan*. New York: Random House, 1998.

Clark, James A. and Michel T. Halbouty. *The Last Boom*. New York: Random House, 1972.

Diamond, Jared. *Guns, Germs, and Steel*. New York: W.W. Norton & Co., 1997.

Ehrenreich, Barbara. *Bait and Switch*. New York: Henry Holt and Company, 2005.

Fraser, Steve. *Wall Street: A Cultural History*. London: Faber and Faber, 2005.

Friedman, Milton and Rose Friedman. *Free to Choose*. New York: Harcourt Brace Jovanovich, 1979.

Greene, Jay E. *100 Great Scientists*. New York: Washington Square Press, 1967.

Greene, Jay E. *100 Great Thinkers*. New York: Washington Square Press, 1967.

Gup, Benton E. *Management of Financial Institutions*. Boston: Houghton Mifflin Co., 1984.

Hall, Robert E. and John B. Taylor. *Macroeconomics*. New York: W.W. Norton & Co., 1986.

Hawking, Stephen. *A Brief History of Time*. Toronto: Bantam Books, 1988.

Hayakawa, S.I. *Language in Thought and Action, Fifth Edition*. San Diego: Harcourt Brace Jovanovich, 1990.

Hicks, John D., George E. Mowry, and Robert E. Burke. *The American Nation*. Boston: Houghton Mifflin Company, 1963.

Jones, Robert R. and Gustav L. Seligmann, Jr. *The Sweep of American History, Vol. II*. New York: John Wiley & Sons, 1970.

Leftwich, Richard W. *The Price System and Resource Allocation*. New York: Holt, Rinehart and Winston, 1966.

Lowenstein, Roger. *When Genius Failed*. New York: Random House, 2000.

McConnell, Campbell R. *Economics, Fifth Edition*. New York: McGraw-Hill Book Co., 1972.

Selected Bibliography

Minutaglio, Bill. *First Son*. New York: Three Rivers Press, 1999.

Murray, Charles. *Losing Ground*. New York: Basic Books, 1984.

Reback, Gary L. *Free the Market*. New York: The Penguin Group, 2009.

Ricks, Thomas E. *Fiasco: The American Military Adventure in Iraq*. New York: The Penguin Press, 2006.

Rima, I.H. *Development of Economic Analysis*. Homewood, Illinois: Richard D. Irwin, Inc., 1967.

Roberts, J.M. *History of the World*. New York: Oxford University Press, 1993.

Shapiro, Eli, Ezra Soloman, and William L. White. *Money and Banking, Fifth Edition*. New York: Holt, Rinehart and Winston, Inc., 1968.

Sorkin, Andrew Ross. *Too Big To Fail*. New York: Viking, 2009.

Sulzberger, C.L. *The American Heritage Picture History of World War II*. New York: American Heritage Publishing Company, Inc., 1966.

Wright, Lawrence. *The Looming Tower*. New York: Vintage, 2006.

Index

A

Afghanistan War, 131–132, 134, 144
Age of Delusion, 97–101
Age of Denial, 109–111
AIG, 154–155
American Business Model, 16, 97–98
American Recovery and Reinvestment Act, 173–174
anti-government ideology, 201–205, 228–231
Apple Computer, 189
Argentina, 188
Arkin, William M., 145
Asia, 183–186

B

baby boomers, 72, 98–99
bailouts, 137, 155, 164–165
bankruptcies, 155–156, 161–162
banks and banking, 36–37, 39–43, 151–153
Bank of England, 34
Baxter, William F., 135
Bear Stearns, 154
Bernanke, Ben, 154
Bin Laden, Osama, 132, 178
Boesky, Ivan, 136
Brazil, 189
Buffet, Warren, 76n, 214–215
Bush, George H.W., 131, 133, 138–139, 204
Bush, George W., 132–133, 143–149, 204–205
business cycle, 85–93

C

capital gains tax, 211–212
capitalism, 183–186. *See also* free-market economy
Carter, Jimmy, 109–110, 138–139, 159–160, 171
Center for Army Lessons Learned (CALL), 127
Chalabi, Ahmed, 133
Chicago School of Economics, 135
China, 17, 183–185
Clinton, William Jefferson, 139–141, 204
Cold War, 125–128
collateralized debt obligations (CDO), 151–152
commercial banks, 36–37, 49–50
communism, 125–128
Community Reinvestment Act (CRA), 159–160
competition in the global economy, 100–101, 106–107, 183–189
conservatives, 118–121, 199, 203
Consumer Financial Protection Bureau (CFPB), 177–178
consumer spending, 9–13
credit card lending, 161–162
credit default swaps (CDSs), 152

D

deficit
    and Bush, George H.W., 138–139
    and Bush, George W., 144
    and Clinton, 140
    and the Great Depression, 89–90
    and the Great Recession, 157
    and increase in government services, 208, 210
Democrats, 133, 139–140, 171–172, 175, 202, 205

depression, 87–93, 118, 201–202, 225
deregulation, 111, 136–137, 139, 149, 203
derivatives, 53–55, 152
Dien Bien Phu, 125
diplomacy and limited resource strategy (DLR), 128–130, 134, 179
diseconomies of large scale, 80–82
distribution, 115–121
Dust Bowl, 88

E
East Texas Oil Field, 104
economic development
    overview, 3–7
    restoring the economy, 193–197
economic equilibrium, 13, 18, 22, 24, 195, 227
economic history
    generally, 3–8, 95–96
    competition in the global economy, 100–101, 106–107, 183–189
    the early years and the Age of Delusion, 97–101
    the 1970s, 103–107
    the Age of Denial, 109–112
economic investment, 50–53
economic models, 15–20
economic optimization, 191–197
economic stimulus, 172–174
economic world. *See* global economy
economics and finance. *See also* money; taxation
    generally, 27–28
    banking, 36–37, 39–43, 151–153

    the business cycle, 85–93
    entitlements, 57–59
    Fallacy of Composition, 29–31, 105, 116, 224, 227
    the financial sector, 49–55
    gold standard, 33–36
    government efficiency and regulation, 79–84
    insurance, 45–48
    lifetime consumption, 61–67
    mortgage lending, 39–43, 151–153, 163–167
    risk-reward trade-off, 42–43
    taxation, purpose of, 73–77
    unemployment, 85–93, 138, 156–157
    utility and the true value of money, 69–72
    welfare, 57–59, 76–77
education, 18–20, 23–24, 81, 99, 184, 212–213
employment
    in the global economy, 21–25
    importance of, 11–13, 227
    maintaining, 192–193
    not necessary for every person, 4–5
    in the public sector, 23–25
    unemployment, 85–93, 138, 156–157
entitlements, 57–59. *See also specific programs*
equilibrium. *See* economic equilibrium
equity investments, 52
estate tax, 212
European Economic Community (EEC), 186–187

F
Fallacy of Composition, 29–31, 105, 116, 224, 227
Fannie Mae, 163–167

Federal Reserve system, 86–87, 105
FEMA, 47
financial investment, 50-53
financial sector, 49–53. *See also* banks and banking; economics and finance; insurance; mortgage lending
Fineman, Howard, 147
fixed-income investments, 52
Ford, Henry, 3, 219
foreign competition, 100–101, 106–107, 183–189
foreign graduate students, 214
foreign policy, 178–180
France, 17, 186
Frank, Barney, 155
Fraser, Steve, 136
Freddie Mac, 164–165
free-market economy
    and economic equilibrium, 24
    and employment, 227
    and equilibrium, 194–195
    and the Fallacy of Composition, 31
    and the global economy, 21, 100
    inadequacy of, 48, 117
    and lack of regulation, 155, 159, 162–163, 166, 203
    and personal freedom, 120
Friedman, Milton, 120
fuel taxes, 212

G
Gaddafi, Muammar, 179
Ghandi, Mahatma, 119

Geithner, Tim, 154
Germany, 6, 16, 17, 98, 123-124, 186
Gingrich, Newt, 140
Global Business Model, 16–18, 100
global economy
    generally, 1–2
    Asia, 183–186
    competition, 100–101, 106–107, 183–189
    consumer spending, 9–13
    employment, 11–13, 21–25
    European Economic Community, 186–187
    history of, 3–8
    models for economic activity, 15–20
    plutocracy, 187–189
    prosperity, uneven, 15–20
globalization, impact of, 17–19
gold standard, 33–36
Goldman Sachs, 153–154
Goldwater, Barry, 138, 201
Gorbachev, Mikhail, 130–131
Gore, Al, 143
government. *See also* deficit; taxation
    vs. conservatives, 118–121
    debt
        and Bush, George W., 148
        and the global economy, 187
        and the Great Depression, 89
        and ideology, 228
        and increase in government services, 141
    efficiency, 79–84
    functions, 199–201

    regulation, 82–84, 231
    spending, 115–121, 144–146 (*See also specific programs*)
    shutdown, 140, 180
Great Depression, 87–93, 118, 201–202, 225
Great Recession
    generally, 151–153
    and borrowers, 160–163
    business failures, 155–156
    causes of, 159–167
    and CRA, 159-160
    and economic downturn, 157–158
    and Fannie Mae, 163–167
    mortgage defaults, 155–157
    real estate bubble bursts, 153–155
    unemployment, 157
Greece, 187
Greenspan, Alan, 166

H
Hawking, Stephen, 226
health care reform, 174–177
Hispanics, 203
history. *See* economic history
Houston, TX, 29
Hussein, Saddam, 131, 133–134

I
ideology
    generally, 113
    Bush, George H.W., 138–139
    Bush, George W., 143–149

Clinton, 139–140
and the Great Recession, 151–167
and lessons of war, 123–134
Obama, 171, 177-179
and politics, 201–205
Reagan, 110–111, 115, 135
rejecting anti-American ideology, 228–231
tax cuts, distribution, and redistribution, 115–121
income disparity, 51
income effect, 105
India, 184–185
inheritance tax, 212
insurance, 45–48. *See also* Medicare
Insurance Principle, 46–47, 63
investments, 50–53
Iranian hostage crisis, 109
Iraq War, 132–134, 144–146, 178–179
Italy, 187

J
Japan, 16,17, 98, 106–107, 123-124, 183
jobs. *See* employment
Jobs, Steve, 219
Johnson, Lyndon B., 125, 201–202
J.P. Morgan, 154

K
Katrina (hurricane), 146–149
Kennedy, John F., 121
Keynesian economic policy, 90
Korean War, 124–126
Kuwait, 131

L

Latin America, 187–189
Lehmann Brothers, 155
liberals, 119
lifetime consumption, 61–67
Long-Term Capital Management (LTCM), 166
Low Labor Cost Model, 16

M

marginal propensity to consume (MPC), 71–72
market economy. *See* free-market economy
McCain, John, 170
Medicare, 62–65, 67, 145–146, 202, 213, 230
Medicare Advantage, 64–65, 213
Mexico, 188
Milken, Michael, 136
Mississippi River Flood of 1927, 88
money
    creation by commercial banks, 36–37
    development of, 5–7
    the gold standard, 33–36
    investment, 50–53
    redistribution, 115–121, 195–196
    true value of, 69–72
moral hazard, 154–155
mortgage-backed securities (MBSs), 163, 176
mortgage crisis, 153–157, 159–167, 176–177
mortgage lending, 39–43, 151–153, 163–167
Murray, Charles, 76, 219

N

NASA, 4
nation, defining, 217–218
national debt. *See* government
National Flood Insurance Program, 47–48
Natural Resource Model, 15
necessities, 7–11
negative multiplier effect, 11–12, 22, 31, 89, 209
Newton, Isaac, 225–226
9/11 terrorist attacks, 131–133, 144, 208
Nixon, Richard, 103, 120
North American Free Trade Agreement (NAFTA), 140
North Korea, 124-125
North Vietnam, 109

O

Obama, Barack, 169–180
Objectivism, 148
OPEC oil embargo, 103–106

P

Paradox of Thrift, 30
Patient Protection and Affordable Care Act, 175–176
Paulsen, Hank, 154
paying the bills, 207–215
Perot, Ross, 103
personal freedom, 120–121
physics, history of, 225–227
plutocracy, 187–189
politics, 199–205. *See also* Democrats; Republicans
poverty, 7, 70–72, 116, 119, 191, 203, 209, 219–220

Priest, Dana, 145
progressives. *See* Democrats
prosperity, 15–20, 219
public policies, 218–221
public service program, 214

Q
al-Qaeda, 129, 131–134, 178

R
Rand, Ayn, 148
Reagan, Ronald, 110–111, 118–121, 135–138, 171, 202–204
real estate bubble, 153–155, 159
Reback, Gary, 135
recession, 91–92. *See also* Great Recession
redistribution, 115–121, 195–196
regulation, 82–84, 231. *See also* deregulation
Republicans, 118, 133, 138–140, 143–148, 172–180, 201–205
Resolution Trust Corporation (RTC), 137, 139
restoring the economy, 193–197
risk-reward trade-off, 42–43
Rita (hurricane), 29
Rockefeller, Nelson, 139
Romney, Mitt, 175
Roosevelt, Franklin, 89, 118, 201
Rubin, Robert, 166

S
sacrifice, 207

Saudi Arabia, 6, 15, 20
savings and loan bailout, 137
Say's Law, 90–91, 192, 194
Simpson, Allen, 208
Social Security, 65–67, 201, 230–231
Sorkin, Andrew Ross, 154
South Korea, 124-125, 183
Soviet-Afghan War, 128–130
Soviet Union, 130–132
stagflation, 105
stimulus, 172–174
student loans, 213

T
Taliban, 129, 132
Taylor, Frederick W., 3
taxation
    adequate, 207–215
    progressive, 72, 74–75, 116, 196
    purpose of, 73–77, 200
    simplification, 75
    tax cuts
        and Bush, George W., 144–146, 208, 211
        and economic activity, 194, 204
        and ideology, 111, 115–121
territorial wars, 125, 131–132, 134
Texas, 20
Third Way, 139–140, 166
Troubled Asset Relief Program (TARP), 155, 159, 177
Turner, Frederick Jackson, 97

U

unemployment, 85–93, 138, 156–157
United Kingdom, 17, 186
utility, 69–72

V

Value-Added Model, 16
Vietnam War, 103, 109, 120, 125–128

W

war
    generally, 134
    Afghanistan War, 131-132, 134, 144
    Cold War, 125–128
    Iraq War, 132–134, 144–146, 178–179
    Korean War, 124–125
    Soviet-Afghan War, 128–130
    Vietnam War, 103, 109, 120, 125–128
    World War II, 90, 98–101, 123–125, 173
Watergate, 103, 120
Watt, James, 3
"weak anthropic principle," 226
wealth, 51, 53, 69–72, 76, 116, 192–196
welfare, 57–59
welfare state vs. welfare society, 76–77
Wolff, Edward, 196
work. *See* employment
World War II, 90, 98–101, 123–125, 173

Z

al Zawahiri, Ayman, 132

About the Author

Michael Gilbert's primary interests in economics are in the related areas of human survival in a modern complex economy, and in the proper relationship of government to private sector activity. He has been a geophysicist since 1974, has taught mathematics at the college and community college level, and has done income tax preparation for many hundreds of people. He has graduate degrees in mathematics and business administration. Michael is an emeritus member of both the American Mathematical Society and the Mathematical Association of America. He is also a member of Beta Gamma Sigma, the national business honor society.